Gevorg Emin

SEVEN SONGS ABOUT ARMENIA

Sovetakan Grogh
Publishers
Yerevan - 1983

Translated from the Armenian
by **MKRTICH SOGHIKIAN**

Edited by
JOAN BATLER

Illustrations by
ANDRANIK KOCHAR

Designed by
VAHAN KOCHAR

© Sovetakan Grogh Publishers
Translated into English
Yerevan 1983

Here are seven songs about my country, Armenia, which has been instilled with new life. Seven is a number which has been hallowed by time — a magic number associated with fairy-tales and miracles... And all I now wish to tell you is indeed like a fairy-tale:

In the distant, and especially the recent past, Armenia has witnessed so many wonders that even an ordinary. account of them seems like a song.

But perhaps you think this is only my yersonal opinion? Nobody who has visited Armenia would disagree with me.

"If I were to be asked where on the planet Earth one can see the most incredible wonders, I would first of all say — Armenia...", said Rockwell Kent.

And a century ago Byron said that the country of Armenians would always remain one of the countries most rich in wonders in the world.

What does our country mean to us?

It means our people and history, land, water, stones, factories, books and our songs. But our country is marked, first and foremost, by the time in which our land has flourished more than ever before. This new era has instilled life in everything that has existed for centuries.

Not only the Armenian people but also its land, water, stones, factories and songs — glorify this newly given life in songs.

So, let's listen to them:

SONG
ABOUT THE
CENTURY

For centuries now — from Ara the Beautiful to Avarair and Sardarapat, we have triumphed by dying, but now we believe that we can and must triumph by living.

The centuries have swept over this land, each leaving scars and wrinkles on the face and in the hearts of our people.

The centuries have gone by and left vestiges for us, such as cuneiform inscriptions, ruined monuments and fortresses.

All of Armenia is like an open-air museum where you can make a practical study of the history of our people and its land, starting from the legendary Noah's Ark down to the actual ruins left by the Turkish janizaries a few decades ago.

Each century has left not only ruins and scars, but has marked a step on the long steep stairway which our people has climbed through misery toward joy.

Which page of the living history of Armenia shall we open first?

If you like, we could start with this mossy stone on which we happen to be standing. Quite possibly it is a fragment of a Hittite or Arameic inscription or a chipping from an Urartian fortress.

It used to be customary to begin the history of our land with Urartu, that is, in about 1000 B.C.

However, the excavations, which have recently taken place in Metsamor, Shengavit and Mokhrablur confirm that our history, in fact, began five thousand years earlier.

But it is not the historical date but the essence and significance of the unearthed ancient monuments that matter most. For example, the ancient metal casting foundry and the hieroglyphs excavated at Metsamor may yet reveal new secrets. They undoubtedly testify to the existence in this land of one of the most ancient civilizations of the world which began long before the legendary Flood.

There are many Urartian fortresses in Armenia, including those at Tushpa (Tosp, Van) and Argishtkhinili (Armavir), the ancient settlements on the shores of Lake Sevan and the fortresses at Teishebaini and Erebuni (the site of present-day Yerevan and its vicinity).

First of all, we should say that in spite of the research carried out by highly-qualified historians and other specialists, many facts about Uraratu have still to be

substantiated and are at times too contradictory to determine, for instance, how long the state existed or what its geographical contours were.

This enigma becomes even more profound when one remembers that the history of Urartu has much in common with that of Armenia, for example, the name of the founder of the Urartu state — Aram or Arame — and the name of the country itself — Urartu, which, according to an ancient inscription, is a misspelling of the word Ararat.

Our folk tales begin with the phrase: "Once there was or was not...", thus emphasising the *content* of the narration without taking responsibility for its *authenticity*.

So, did the powerful state of Urartu actually exist, or is it simply a misspelling of the word "Ararat"?

Leaving it up to historians to determine this, let us relate the facts and various opinions which are discussed and often disputed today.

Urartu, one of the most powerful and highly developed powers of the ancient world, which covered the territory of Armenia of the past, was founded in the 9th-10th century B. C. and existed until the 6th century B.C. when its capital, Tushpa, was totally destroyed.

Before the formation of the Urartian state, this territory was inhabited by the ancestors of the Armenian tribes who called their country Nairi (this possibly explains the expressions found in Urartian cuneiforms, such as "we came, conquered and captured", referring to various parts of Armenia).

Like Armenia, subsequently, the history of Nairi began

ith sufferings and disasters. Here is an extract from a cuneiform of the Assyrian king, Tiglat-Palassar I (1115—1077) about his invasion of the country of Nairi: "a vast and unknown country which has never been subjugated" ..."I captured their largest towns and confiscated their possessions. I destroyed their settlements by fire and turned them into heaps of ruins and wastelands. I seized their herds of horses, mules and cows and their agricultural implements and took them away..." ("Took them away"— what a discreet way of describing violence and destruction!).

The founder of the Urartu state and its first king was Arame or Aram (860—843 B.C.). His name has been preserved in Armenian pagan legends and tales and obvioulsy explains why foreign peoples subsequently began calling our people or one of its tribes Aramens or Armens and the country *Arme*.

The Urartu State was originally formed on the territory around Lake Biaina (now Lake Van in Western Armenia), and for this reason the Urartians called their country *Biainili*.

Incidentilly, information about the country of Urartu (referred to as *Ararat* and *Alarod*) is also to be found in the Bible, which states that the sons of king Sinakherib (Senekerim) of Assyria fled to the country of Ararat after killing their father.

According to Movses Khorenatsi, these sons, Adramelek and Sanasar, settled near the present-day town of Sassoun. There undoubtedly is an indirect link between the tes-

Panorama of Yerevan

timonies of the Bible, Movses Khorenatsi and The Dare-devils of Sassoun, connecting the construction of the fortress of Sassoun in the epic with the name of the warrior Sanasar.

Later, during the reign of King Menua and Argishti I, the borders of Urartu extended over the present-day Ararat Valley and the shores of Lake Sevan.

It was namely during the reign of Rusa II a canal was dug which irrigates the vineyards around Yerevan to this day. "I dug a canal from the River Ildaruni (now the Hrazdan river flowing through Yerevan) and planted vineyards", boasted Rusa II, attributing to himself the toil of the Armenian-Urartian peasants.

To understand their truly back-breaking work, one only has to remember that this canal (like the Akanates Canal at Ashtarak) was dug through rocks and its rocky underground sections were sometimes three hundred metres long.

Let us have a look at the Urartian fortresses and settlements.

The Cyclopean fortresses contain huge concave clay vessels which in turn contain grains of wheat and grape pips.

Scattered around them are rusty swords and lances, statuettes of gods and idols and women's jewellery.

Thirty or fourty centuries ago our ancestors built fortresses in this land, cultivated wheat and vines. defended their crops from foreign invaders, worshipped their gods and idols and transformed their love and sufferings into works of art.

They dug Cyclopean canals but these canals irrigated the lands of the Urartian kings.

They grew vines and sowed wheat but their crops were confiscated by the Urartian kings and stored in huge barns. "We toiled much but gained nothing in return". These words, which sound like a line from a hymn during the epoch of slavery were inscribed by unknown masters on the mosaic in the Temple of Garni.

And when Urartian gods and idols demanded offerings, the most beautiful daughters and the finest sons of the peasants and artisans were sacrificed before the altars.

When the Urartian kings wanted to found the fortress of Erebuni, it was again the peasants and artisans who dragged the stones and moulded the clay for the fortress; it was they who carved on the stone cuneiforms which over 2750 years ago heralded the birth of the town of Erebuni (Yerevan) to the world (and which have been preserved to this day in the museums of new Yerevan).

"With the might of the god of Khaldians,
I, Argishti, the son of Menua,
Built this solid fortress-town.
And named it Erebuni,
In glory of the country of Biaina.
And to the terror of her enemies..!
Argishti declares — this land was barren,
I built huge fortifications here,
With the might of the god of Khaldians,
Argishti, the son of Menua,

2—Seven songs about Armenia

Is the mighty king of the country of Biaina,
And overlord of the town of Tushpa..."

Then another Rusa, Sardur and Argishti took the peasants and artisans away from their settlements, gave them lances and spears instead of spades and looms and ordered them to attack the northern tribes.

From Lake Biaina they got as far as blue Lake Sevan, built fortresses on its shores and carved inscriptions on enormous rocks in glory of the victory of the Urartian kings.

For the victory celebrations they caught in Lake Sevan the "king of fish"— the famous trout whose scales are covered with red spots, symbolising, as it were, the drops of blood shed by the Armenian people.

And when bellicose Assyria declared war the frightened Urartu kings fled the country, the peasants and artisans defended this land, which did not as yet belong to them, with their blood.

They pursued the mighty Assyrian kings to Nineveh and Babylon and the "hanging gardens" of Queen Semiramis.

The people fought, suffered and dreamed...

And what has been handed down from them to us? Cuneiforms which only glorify King Rusa or Argishti; fortresses which immortalize the glory of Sardur; cyclopean canals whose construction is attributed to Queen Semiramis.

But why go back so far in time? Only recently during the construction of the Assuan Dam in Egypt, four gigantic identical statues of Pharaoh Ramses were found. Underneath the gigantic statues of the tyrant thousands of peasants and artisans once built the Sphinx and the Pyramid of Cheops and relatively recently the Assuan Dam...

The gigantic statues of the tyrant were given false credit for the peoples talent and hard work.

But what has remained of the people who laboured, created and fought? The four statues of Ramses, the names of Sardur, Rusa and Semiramis have been preserved in history but we have no evidence of the rightful owner of this lands and true creator of history — the *people*.

I was pondering over this when the retreating waters of mirror-like Lake Sevan revealed cuneiform inscriptions on the lake and my thoughts took the form of a poem:

> The Lake calmly floats and wavers and shines,
> And the rocks appear with cuneiform signs...
> "I am king Rusa, son of Argishti,
> The monarch of feats, truly believe me,
> I fought, conquered lands and reigned as a cult,
> I built..."
>
> No, you cheat, you native of Khald!
> You'd better tell us of your throngs of slaves,
> Who were forced to build your splendid fortress,
> Who, though never stopped to hate you to death,
> Made you an idol void of any breath,
> Who shook the castles deep into their base,
> And left heir corpses beneath this stone-case,
> Who laboured and carved signs of history...

And the waters wave, clad in mystery,
And the letters lie, the signs are dreary...

The enigmas linked with the origin and formation of any people are complicate and shrouded in mist, and this is especially of the sources of the Armenian people.

The origin of the Armenian people can be traced back into the remote past when nations had still not been historically formed in the greater part of Asia Minor and tribes lived separately or formed bigger unions as, for instance, in the country of Nairi.

The first Armenian state was founded after the fall of Urartu in its territory with the same capital of Tushpa (Tosp, Van).

The Armenian tribes consolidated while the Urartu state was still in existence and by the time Urartu fell, the Armenian people were already able to found an independent state. According to some, all the tribes living in this territory were already speaking the same language — Aremnian.

This explains why an Armenian state emerged *immediately* after the fall of Urartu. For this reason also the ancient tribes and peoples for a long time called us Armenians, Uraratians, and Armenia — the country of Urartu.

In the Behistun cuneiform inscriptions, the Persian king Darius I (522—485 B.C.) was the first to mention the state of Armenia as being "rebellious" and "indomitable". "The country of Armenia" in the text of this old

Persian cuneiform corresponds with the name "Urartu" in the Babylonian texts of that time. (In the Bible the country of Urartu is referred to as Ararat).

After the Behistun inscription the ancient Greeks and Mars called our country *Armenia* and our people, *Armens* after the "Arme" (or "Urume") tribe who lived in the district of Aghtsnik and who in the 8th—7th cc. B.C. invaded Tushpa, the capital of Urartu with the Mars.

Our ancestors called themselves *Hai* and their country *Hayastan,* probably after one of the tribes living in the country of *Hayass,* who later played a decisive role in the formation of the Armenian people with the *Hai* and *Arme* tribes living in Arme-Shupria and Beaynili.

Some historians assert that our people named themselves after our ancestor Haik, about whom we read an ancient legend in the book of the "History of the Armenian People" by the 5th century historian, Movses Khorenatsi. According to this legend, the hero Haik lived with his tribe on vast fertile lands which were, however, at the mercy of the tyrant Bel. For this reason Haik decided to move with all his tribe to the barren mountain crags to gain independence. According to the legend, in this new place there was "a salty lake full of small fish", or Lake Biaina, later called Van.

Enraged by Haik's daring action, Bel attacked him with a vast army but Haik defeated him in an unequal battle and killed the tyrant, ensuring his tribe's right to independence.

This legend anticipated, as it were, the history of our

people; since then Armenia has constantly struggled for her existence in unequal battles against tyrants and invaders, and suffering throughout the centuries, has gradually acquired the secret of longevity.

When the legendary Bel attacked our people, our ancestor Haik killed the marauding tyrant with an arrow from his bow, thus revenging our people.

When Queen Semiramis of Assyria tried to charm Armenia and her king into submission, King Ara the Beautiful chose to fall in battle, defending the honour of his country and wife, Queen Nvard.

The huge elephants of the invading Persian king Hazkert were rebuffed by the brave army general Vardan, indomitable Gevond Yerets and the brilliant chronicler Yeghisheh...

The people fought the pagans with the Christian cross and used the invincible legion of the thirty six letters of their alpahabet against the treacherous Christian Byzantine.

In each war the men died on the battlefields, the young girls and women were taken into captivity, the mothers prayed and the old men comforted them with the hope that the war would soon be over.

How could they know that these wars would go on for thirty centuries and only then the people would at last become free and this land would really be theirs?

Nothing about the wars or the people's sufferings changed — only the names were different of the foreign invaders and "their" leaders who ascribed to themselves the people's talent and courage, the fruits of their labour and military valour.

When this land was invaded by omnipotent Rome, the victories of the Armenian people were celebrated by Tigran the Great and the town and fortress built by the people was named Tigranakert in his honour.

When Rome was succeeded by Parsia and Byzantium, the people's heroism was ascribed to Vagharshak and Arshak and the new towns were named Vagharshapat and Arshakavan.

But some of the wars and invasions threatened the very existence of the people, its language, literature and faith. At times like this the entire people — men, women, old folk and children — arose in arms.

Such was the case in 451 at the battle of Avarair. The elephants of the Persian armies crushed the Armenians' light cavalry, but king Hazkert of Persia was frightened away by the fanatical faith of our people and their devotion to their language, country and freedom.

The centuries came and went, as did new invaders. The centuries passed forever but the scars left by them remained.

Vaguely understanding that their king and Church did not represent their State and beliefs, the Armenians formed heresies with the same fanaticism with which they had formerly believed in religion, organised revolts against the Church and nobility and flung the cauldron of Holy Myron into the abyss.

And although the heretics were branded, tortured and

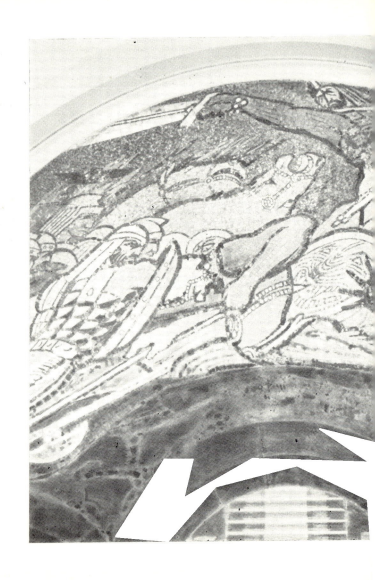

In the hall of Matenadaran

killed, the echo of their uprisings resounded for a long time in the mountains of Armenia and in the people's hearts.

And when the Arabs, Seljuks and Mongols attacked this land, the people, who had totally rejected both religion and atheism, found refuge only in folk tales and created the epic hero David of Sassoun with his lightning sword who was summoned to free the people when its "cup of patience" overflowed.

David already knew that it was not enough to drive out the foreign tax-collectors and cut the Meilk of Msra to pieces. He understood what was most important: he should not destroy the troops of Melik of Msra — the poor Arab peasants who had been forced to fight — because he knew that it was the Arab leaders and not their people who were to blame for the war.

But what happened then?

It is much easier to destroy than it is to build. However, the foreign invaders grew tired of destroying and our people indefatigably went on building.

They built Artashat on the site of ruined Erebuni (Yerevan), Tigranakert on the site of Artashat, Vagharshapat on the site of Tigranakert, and so on and so forth... They built an Armenian fortress on the site of an Urartian one, replaced the pagan temple of Garni with the Christian churches of Etchmiadzin, Zvartnots, Hripsimeh and Akhtamar.

And when invaders rampaged all over the country, the people were forced to hide in caves by the Azat River and to make use of the time available and keeping their weapons sharp they hewed the Church of Geghard out of the rocks. And at night they came out of their caves to water their vineyards at Ashtarak so that the vines, planted when the Urartian state was still in existence, did not perish.

As soon as there was peace for a few years, new towns, such as Ani, full of skilled craftsmen, grew up. The fields and gardens flourished again and new manuscripts and miniatures were written in the monastic cells. And the songs of our *Gussans* (minstrels), at first resounding timidly, became louder and louder; the merry tight rope-walkers and acrobats entertained the people with their amusing tricks and the joyful music of wedding and baptism celebrations sounded everywhere.

Gradually the country became a proper state again. Before the country was ransacked by new invaders and the Armenian people were forced to flee across the world, they founded new schools and colleges of erudition, and built architectural monuments on the slopes of mountains, in valleys and on the shores of lakes in the vast country of Armenia.

For the last time from the 11th to the 14th century our people hoped to have again founded their own country and state on the shores of the Mediterranean, in Cilicia, but it was here that their dream of independence was again buried for many centuries.

Armenia was again invaded by Turkish and Persian tribes who tore the land apart, separating brothers and sisters, and mothers and sons, tearing pens away from parchments and ploughs away from the soil and wiping the name of Armenia off the map. "The invasion of the Turks of Asia Minor and the formation by them of the marauder state of Karahisar was one of the greatest misfortunes of the Middle Ages", wrote Marx about this epoch.

This misfortune lasted for a very long time — five hundred years, to be precise. It lasted so long that our people, who used to be excellent stone masons, started building houses out of clay and mud. The wonderful manuscripts were written in Turkish with Armenian letters, or in Armenian with Persian letters. And our people had to listen to the monotonous shrieks of Mollahs instead of their inimitable melodious chants.

As Lord Byron correctly remarked: "It would be difficult to find so many misfortunes and calamities as those abounding in the history of the Armenian people— people whose deeds are of an exclusively peaceful nature and whose shortcomings have been imposed on them by the will of their conquerors and oppressors".

But whatever happened, how was it conceivable to enslave a people who, by looking at their native mountains learnt to remain standing staunchly, who, by looking at the rigid, straight contours of their architectural monuments, absorbed their beauty and by looking at their cuneiforms and manuscripts, always remembered their origins?

How was it possible to enslave a people who had

created the epic about David of Sassoun, or to take away the faith of a people who had fought at Avarair, or suppress the feelings of a people who had been brought up on the explosive emotions of the poet Grigor Narekatsi, or force new gods and prophets on the descendants of the heretic Zarehavantsi, or take away a language in which the folk-storytellers of Gokhtan and the poets Shnorhali, Frik and Kuchak had written?

However, countless attempts were made to destroy our literature and uproot the great tree of our culture.

But the seeds shaken from it were scattered all over the world. And whereas centres of Armenian culture used only to be found in Armenia, they have now grown up in every part of the world.

Armenia was shaken by uprisings, revolts and stormy clashes with foreign invaders.

Time and again ideas and plans of creating a free and peaceful Armenia arose both in Armenia itself and in the Armenian colonies scattered all over the world. In an Indian colony, for instance, a book appeared which charted the programme of the future liberation of Armenia and its national constitution. In Gharabagh memorable meetings were held by Armenians who looked towards Russia for assistance.

The inspirers and leaders of the national liberation movement, Israel Ori and Hovsep Emin enthusiastically, but without much hope of success, visited European courts, paid homage to Peter the Great, and finally Russian cannons came to the assistance of the Armenian military leader, David Bek, and subsequently, in 1828 the eastern part of Armenia was liberated from the Persian yoke.

The Armenian people rejoiced. The great founder of our new literature, Khachatur Abovian, was delirious with joy, as was Nerses Ashtaraketsi, the wise and brave Catholicos of all Armenians of that time, who rode on his white steed with a sword in one hand and a cross in the other into battle against the Persians under the Russian banner at the head of the Russian and Armenian detachments.

The Russian Decembrists who had defended and fought for our freedom were also overjoyed.

The annexation of Eastern Armenia to Russia not only saved our people from physical extermination but also brought it spiritually closer to the great Russian people, and to the latter's inherent passionate search for truth which was later a source of the revolutionary upheavals.

But while the Decembrist officers were reading illegal poems by Pushkin, and Griboyedov's play *Woe from wit* was being perfomed for the first time in the Sardar fortress in Yerevan, tsarist gendarmes were already deporting the most prominent members of the Armenian intelligentsia to Siberia and a Russian civil servant had already taken the first bribe from an Armenian peasant.

Among the exiled were Nerses Ashtaraketsi who, when the Russian troops arrived at his village, had gone to the cemetery, knelt in front of his father's grave and exclaimed emotionally: "Do you hear, father, the hour you dreamed

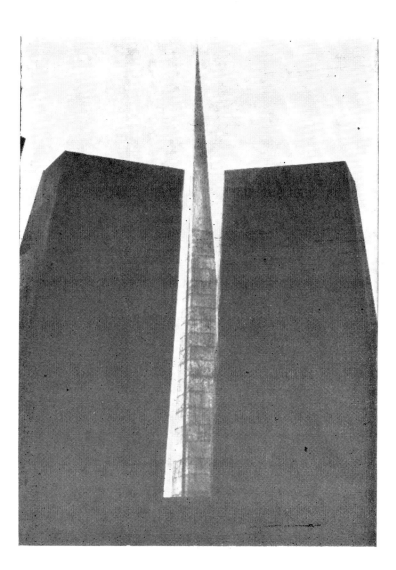

about has come—the Armenian people has been liberated by the Russians".

He was exiled because it was unfortunately not the Russian people who had liberated Armenia but Count Paskievich who had drowned Poland in blood and was a staunch opponent of any people's aspirations towards freedom and whose aim was to get new fodder for the two-headed eagle's claws.

He did not know, and could not know at that time that the people was capable of ripping off both of the eagle's heads.

Whereas Khachatur Abovian had seen and sung the praises of one united Russia, Mikael Nalbandian, a friend and comrade-in-arms of Herzen, Ogaryov and Chernishevsky, later in the sixties already saw another. He knew about the Senate in Russia and the Senate Square which had been stained with the Decembrists' blood, as well as about serfdom and the journal "Kolokol" ("Bell") edited by Herzen, heralding its doom.

Nalbandian did not link our people's hopes of national liberation with tsarist Russia but with the abolishment of autocracy. He already realised that tsarist Russia was a people's prison and that until this prison was destroyed, the Armenian people would not be free.

The only religion which is worth believing in and dying for is freedom, proclaimed Nalbandian. It was not in vain that his famous poem "Liberty" was read by Armenian young people with almost religious reverence:

... I cried out — "Liberty..!"
Let the vicious enemy,
With its firearms and lightnings,
Plot or thunder behind me...

Ev'n if dragged up to the rope,
To the gallows shameful, dirty,—
I shall never, never stop
Crying out — "Liberty..."

The seeds of Marxism, which were at that time being disseminated in Russia by Plekhanov, Lenin and his comrades-in-arms, fell on this fertile soil.

And it is not fortuitous that from the very start many eminent members of Armenian society became Lenin's close friends and comrades-in-arms. The Samara group was the first Marxist group to emerge in Armenia and it remained loyal to Lenin to the end of his days. Many Armenians, who are remembered to this day, struggled for the Revolution's victory in Samara, Moscow, Petrograd, Paris, Poland, Switzerland, Baku, Tbilisi and in Armenia itself.

But before the day awaited by them dawned, a cruel darkness descended on the Armenian land and her people.

... Whereas the people of Eastern Armenia had been saved in 1828 from physical extermination and religious oppression, Western Armenia had for several centuries been groaning under the yoke of Turkish tyranny.

The Western Armenians had been deprived of all their human rights, property and freedom of religion and

—33—

3—Seven songs about Armenia

subjected daily to robbery, oppression and religious persecution.

In these dreadful times the western Armenians considered that their brothers who had been "liberated by a Christian king" were truly fortunate, and dreamed of the day when they too, would be saved by the Russians.

Their national liberation movement and revolts (whether in Zeitun, the Sassoun mountains or in any other place), their open love of Russians and sympathy for Russia could not but arouse the boundless hatred of a despot such as Sultan Hamid.

Every now and then the Turkish butchers drowned the Armenian liberation movement in a blood bath, waiting for a suitable occasion to deal a mortal blow on the Armenian people as a whole.

And this occasion soon appeared...

In the spring of 1915, screening themselves behind the so-called war-aime laws, the Young Turks who governed Turkey at that time, cold-bloodedly deported and exterminated the western Armenians on a mass scale, in the same way as subsequently the German fascists tried to do with the Slavs, Jews and other peoples of Europe.

Pan-Turkism, the Young Turks' fiendish programme differed only slightly from the German militarists' Pangermanism.

In both cases what concerned them most was to conquer the whole world and annihilate a certain people. The only difference was that the Pan-turks sought to exterminate the Armenian people and 'by forcing the

Russians out of the Caucasus, annexing this region to Turkey and turning the Black Sea into an internal Turkish sea to create the great Turan from the shores of the Bosphorus to Lake Baikal', whereas the German fascists sought to create 'a great German Empire as far as the Urals' and in doing so they intended to exterminate all the Slav peoples.

Following a carefully-devised plan, the Turks confiscated the property of the Armenians, deported them from their towns and villages and armed henchmen took them in separate groups to death camps in the deserts of Ter-Zor in Mesopotamia. The German fascists would most likely have not been pleased with their work because there were no gas chambers, large crematoria, Auschwitz 'bathhouses' or intellectual butchers reading *Mein Kampf* by the light of lamps made of human skin.

What's more, in contrast to the sophistically-equipped camps at Auschwitz and Buchenwald, in the desert of Ter-Zor the fine long plaits of tortured girls and women were not put to good use and the unburied rotting corpses jeopardised the assassins' health. In the summer and autumn of 1915 dreadful epidemics broke out in many Turkish vilayets and especially in the army. Yes, the means of extermination were indeed primitive but as brutal as those of the German fascist murderers were later to be. It was also of a kind of janisary barbarity.

Many Armenian writers, scientists and composers were stoned to death...

At this time the only light in Turkey came from the

fires set alight by petrol in which Armenian women danced their dance of death at gun point, but this light only intensified the medieval gloom which had descended upon the country.

Three and a half million Armenians lived in Western Armenia before the Genocide organised first by Sultan Hamid and then by the Young Turks.

The Turkish assassins deported and exteminated about two million Armenians; the rest, who had miraculously remained alive, fled abroad. Most of them settled in the Lebanon, Syria, France, Egypt, Greece, Iran, North and South America.

A settled ancient people once lived in its land. A bloodthirsty yataghan cut it down at its roots and divided it into two terrible halves — a people with land and a land without people.

The Turkish henchmen not only planned their dreadful crime beforehand, but took steps to ensure the world did not find out about it.

However, this monstrous crime shook the whole world. A wave of protest rolled from one country to another — from Uruguay to Iran, from Russia to Iceland, from England to Italy, from Greece to Norway, from India to Switzerland and Canada...

Many eminent twentieth-century politicians, scientists, artists and writers condemned the Young Turks' unprecedented crime, spoke out in the defence of the Armenian people and expressed their sympathy. They included

Gladstone, Nansen, Gorky, Bryusov, France, Fores, Morgenthau, Pineau, Vegner, Toynbee, Kalarov, Lenin, Liebknecht, Kirov and Ordjonikidze.

Many Communist and Socialist parties passed resolutions on these events, The *Pravda* newspaper angrily condemned the Young Turks' bloody crime and the Central Committee of the Bulgarian Communist Party tabled a special resolution on the account.

The atrocities of the Young Turks were also condemned by a number of Turkish public figures, including Nazim Bey himself an eye-witness and a participant of the massacres; Fifat Mevlan Zadeh, Ali Kemal, Refid Khalid and others...

These atrocious crimes, which blackened the reputation of Turkey, were also violently condemned by one of the greatest Turkish poets of our century — Nazim Hikmet, in his poem *An Evening Stroll:*

> ... Suren, the grocer, then switched the light on,
> In his grocery, and pondered alone...
> He couldn't forget the Armenians slain,
> Nor could he forgive in his mind and brain,
> His father's butchers,— he couldn't do that,
> He would have to hate..!
> And yet he loves you, since he surely knows,
> You had never thought of blessing all those,
> Who had stamped one day that brand of disgrace
> Upon Turkey's face..!

Perhaps the Young Turks never expected this worldwide wave of protests? Perhaps they weren't fully aware

of the enormity of their crime, or, perhaps, had never thought of its monstrous proportions and consequences?

Alas, this is not true. And herein lies the most cynical part of their crime.

Five years prior to the terrible events of 1915, they scrupulously planned and anticipated not only all the details of the Armenian Genocide, but also the worldwide public reaction and its ineffectiveness:

In 1910, at the Congress of Young Turks held at Salonika, Dr. Nazim, one of the leaders of the party, explaining the positive and negative effects of the Genocide on Turkey, noted: "... It is beyond doubt that after the Armenian massacres, a huge wave of indignation and protests will spread everywhere; and Turkey's moral prestige will be dealt a heavy blow..."

And then he hastily consoled his listeners by saying: "But one shouldn't forget that it won't last long, and *everything is bound to be forgotten soon...*"

What a savage cynicism lies behind his words! He attempted to put to use even the best and most noble human qualities — placability, generosity and magnanimity to forget old wounds — at the service of the assassins!

Yes, not only disgusting cynicism lurks behind these words, but, unfortunately, a sound understanding of our world in which for centuries peoples have been mere tools in the hands of their rulers.

So much so, in fact, that one wouldn't expect anybody to come to the aid of a small, disintegrating people at a time when egotism was the sole mechanism used in the relations between countries; at a time when every government was only worried about its own interests, profits and natural reserves, which were dearer than the blood of the Armenian people.

"Everything is bound to be forgotten soon..." This was all the Turkish assassins were callously counting upon...!

And 25 years after the Armenian massacres another assassin by the name of Adolf Hitler relied on the same sort of "forgetfulness" when sending his SS butchers to invade Poland' "Wipe out all men, women and children without mercy! What counts most is brutality and speed! *Everything will be forgotten soon! Who recalls the Armenian massacres nowadays...?*

Unfortunately, he was right: only 25 years afterwards nobody remembered the Armenian massacres! The new fascist assassins, encouraged by the forgetfulness of mankind and the impunity enjoyed by the butchers, were free to replace Ter-Zor and Meskench with Buchenwald and Dachau. They thought they had the right to slaughter and their techniques of killing people had greatly expanded: six million Russians, Czechs, Poles and Jews instead of just two million Armenians were killed!

But they forgot it was not 1915 but 1945. Times had changed with the emergence of the mighty country of the Soviets which was destined to throw fascism to its grave..!

Before long, Berlin, the henchmens' lair was stormed by the Armenian troops, as well, who had neither forgotten the old crimes against mankind or the new brutalities.

Indeed, both the Turkish assassins and the German fascists were totally wrong in presuming that human placability could equally be applied to such an unforgivable crime as the Genocide...

And it was no mere chance that in 1964, when the war-mongers in Bonn, counting on the same human "forgetfulness" attempted to stop the judicial prosecution of the fascist murderers on the grounds that the crimes were outdated, progressive people of the world firmly opposed them.

There can be no forgetfulness, no leniency in punishing the culprits of such appalling crimes. The assassins had to bear full responsibility for the crimes committed regardless of time. This decree, announced on March 4, 1965, by the USSR Supreme Soviet expressed the will of all nations of the world.

All that remained in Eastern Armenia after the holocaust of 1915 was a handful of refugees and orphans — one tenth of our people living on one tenth of our territory.

It seemed as if everything had been lost; everything had been reduced to ashes, dusty ruins and graves in what had once been known as the country of Armenia!

It seemed as if this ancient people, who had given the world the treasures of its ancient culture, had been wiped off the face of the earth in only three or four years!

It seemed as if the savage duel between man and beast had ended in favour of the beast, the struggle between light and medieval gloom, in favour of gloom...

The Armenian people had been deserted by all their 'allies' and 'friends' and had been left ali alone in the world!

"We should like to help Armenia", exclaimed English politicians hypocritically, "but how can we when our ships cannot climb to the top of Mount Ararat?"

However, there was a ship in the world by the name of *'Avrora'* which would soon come to the rescue of our people choking in a sea of blood...

The Turkish assassins were terribly wrong to believe that by committing this crime they could wipe out Armenia and the Armenian people although after the Genocide of 1915, they made a second attempt by carrying out bloody massacres in Baku and Eastern Armenia until 1920!

They did not and could not understand that a people is not measured by the *size* but by its *quality*...

The blazing fires of the holocaust and the blood shed by the Genocide *inflamed* and *tempered* our suffering people to the point of being undefeatable and infractable. The enormous physical and spiritual pressure crushed them and made them as hard as diamonds. Our people contracted like a spiral which accumulates enormous force for stretching itself out...

The Genocide had killed, if one might put it so, the very substance of our people, but gave strength to their *spirit*. One eye-witness of the crime was fully justified in saying later that the Turkish assassins succeeded in killing the substance, but failed to deal with its essence..

Yes, only 700 000 Armenians were left to live on the small plot of land known as present-day Armenia.

But they were a people who, through age-old suffering, had acquired the secret of resurrection.

You see, our people had to endure atrocities throughout their history.In captivity they retained their dignity, when defeated they knew they had triumphed and when dying they knew they would go on living...

To have an idea of the mythical phoenix, which is said to rise out of its ashes after being consumed by fire, one should look at the Armenian people! And whoever does not believe in the legend of the Resurrection, should visit Armenia!

Dying rather then living, we not only continued to survive, but also to create, struggle and live in hope...!

Our fire was always glowing even when we seemed to have been buried under ashes!

And if at times we had to keep silent, we did so in the way our ancestor Haik had done — with his bow strained before firing the mortal arrow!

Even in times of the most dreadful danger, the world not only heard our immortal songs, but also the fearful thunder of our battle-cry of liberty resounding from Avarair to Tsura castle, from Zeitoun to the top of Mt. Moussa and the plane of Sardarapat!

Yes, after the Genocide only 700,000 Armenians were left in Eastern Armenia, but they had suffered much and knew how to defy the enemy as courageously as Haik, how to love as tenderly as Ara, how to accept a martyr's death as bravely as Vardan, how to create spiritual light as wisely as Mashtots, how to build Zvartnotses and how to murmur the prayers of Narek. And before long, this devastated country of annihilated people gave the rest of the world the melodies of Aram Khachaturian, the magic rainbow of colours of Martiros Sarian, the glittering silver domes of the Byurakan Observatory and pink-stoned Yerevan and the viorant poems of Charents:

> ...And now here I am...
> On the mountains of my ruined land,
> Standing firm and strong,
> With luck in my hand,
> Creating my songs,
> My thunderous songs which are being hurled
> To all continents all over the world,
> Wherever peoples suffer in distress...
> ... My soul is now a radio-station,
> Which is being watched throughout the world,
> A soaring station,
> Mighty and awesome,
> As mount Massis...

Yes, only 700 thousand Armenians were left, but this meant one million and four hundred thousand skilful hands. And only a few decades later Armenia began delivering the most elaborate and sophisticated and precision machinery to more than 80 countries of the world (including... Turkey!) and some of the intricate instruments made in Armenia have been sent to the stars and the Moon on board Soviet spaceships.

In a few decades these 700,000 Armenians have become

about three million and have built a powerful, new Armenia on the heaps of ashes and ruins, which is the best monument to the victims of 1915 and the heaviest tombstone to have been laid on the barbaric schemes of all the various assassins of our people.

From the very start of World War II all the Armenian people did all they could in the sacred struggle of liberation against fascism. They even did what seemed impossible by producing Admiral Hovanness Isakov from their arid stony land.

Our small peace-loving people contributed generals and marshals and all kinds of troops to this war. They included, to name but a few, Marshal Hovhannes Baghramian, Air Marshal Armenak Khamperiants, and Marshal Babadjanian in the artillery and armoured troops...

In World War II the entire Armenian people — both in Soviet Armenia and in exile displayed tremendous valour. Over a third of our small people participated in the battles against fascism and hundreds of thousands lost their lives. Tens of thousands of Armenians living abroad struggled against German fascism not only within the ranks of the allied troops but in the partisan detachments and resistance movements, prisons and concentration camps all over Europe and Africa.

The heroes and martyrs of that sacred war of liberation included the Armenian poet Misak Manushian, the famous hero and leader of the International Brigade in Paris; Hermine Razgratlian (Sashka) the 19 year-old partisan girl in Bulgaria hung by the Germans; Luiza

The Bells of Liberty of Sardarapat

Aslanian (Las) the woman writer condemned to death in the fascist concentration camp, and many other thousands.

Characteristically, the German fascists failed to persuade even the Armenian prisoners-of-war who had been subjected to torture and hunger in the fascist concentration camps, in which the last glimmers of indomitability and resistance had supposedly been crushed, to fight against our country.

When the first battalion of Armenian prisoners-of-war, assembled by the Germans at Pulava, one of the concentration camps in Poland, was brought to the front line and the fascists made arousing speeches and fallacious statements, and then ordered them to fight against their countrymen, the Armenians rebelled under the leadership of Issahak Andreasian, a Red Army officer, and joined our troops fighting heroically and inflicting heavy casualties on the Germans...

Once bitten, twice shy, the Germans no longer dared to bring other battalions of Armenian prisoners of war close to the front line and instead sent them to France.

In France they immediately joined the French partisans and energetically fought against the Germans and in recognition of their feats, General de Gaule in person presented the highest awards of France to them.

According to the press of many European countries, the Armenians were among the staunchest and bravest fighters against fascism. The Armenians, you see, unlike other peoples, had already felt the dreadful danger of emerging fascism in 1915.

The German fascists were also well aware of this, and it was no mere coincidence that in his infamous "Green File" Goering warned the fascist assassins to take into account the special hatred of the Armenians for them when they arrived in the Caucasus...

Yes, the Armenians certainly did hate the German militarists.

During World War I Young Turks were the Germans' allies and the "civilized" Germans not only failed to hold back their hands, but also spared no effort in whetting Taleat's and Enver's Pan-Turkist appetites by promising to grant them new territories in the Caucasus at the expense of Russia.

"The method is Prussian, the execution — Turkish", wrote historians and eyewitnesses of the 1915 massacres, noting the disgraceful participation of German militarists in the crime.

It was because of this "special hatred" that the Armenians, although dispersed all over the world, spared no effort whatsoever in their fight against fascism. They knew full well that the victory won against fascism would be a victory over all types of fascism, a victory upon which the fate of all peoples depended, including that of the Armenian people and their homeland which they longed to return to...

There is profound and instructive historic significance in the fact that this dream could only come true after the victorious conclusion of World War II.

4—Seven songs about Armenia

It was this great historic victory over German fascism that saved the victims of Turkish fascism — the Armenian refugees scattered all over the world — and offered them every possibility of returning to their beloved homeland...

More then 200,000 Armenians (about 300,000 at present) have returned to Armenia from almost every corner of the world in the last few years, thus increasing the rate of its progress and renaissance with their dedicated labour...

Hero, witness, martyr, victim — these words crop up more often than any others in Armenian history books.

The Armenian people has known many courageous patriotic heroes who have been immortalized in legends and songs. This is true, for instance, of Ara the Beautiful, our first hero who was alive when Armenia was first formed; of Vardan Mamikonian the hero of the war of 451 against Persian invaders, and numerous heroes, known and unknown, of the Battle of Sardarapat in 1918 when a handful of Armenian survivors of the massacre stopped the Turkish hordes from destroying Russian Armenia.

But there is a strange and tragic truth about all the heroes of Armenia; without exception they all triumphed by dying!

Ara the Beautiful *defeated* Queen Semiramis of Assyria *by dying;* Vardan the Brave and the other heroes of Avarair *triumphed by dying* and not long ago we *won* the battle of Sardarapat by *dying...*

And, unfortunately, our history itself has never offered

us any other possibility, so we had to choose death to win a victory.

Christian heroism has become an inalienable law of our history; our death has become the inevitable precondition of our victory and of our very existence to such an extent that even the idea of triumphing and living, or rather the very idea of being able to win by living is regarded by us as something of a crime.

This strange and unusual idea needs a long time to fundamentally alter this kind of heroism which has been hallowed by time and recognised as the only feature of our patriotism. Inspiring words leading our people to their destruction must now be replaced by deeds which, though outwardly unobstrusive, can *really* help safeguard our people.

Yes, our people has died and risen again many times during its age-old tortuous history...

But after the massacre of 1915, torn apart by the Turks and drenched in blood, our people not only didn't die, and not only went on living but was *reborn*.

A fine, powerful country with a rich culture created in just a few decades on heaps of ashes and rubble — doesn't this sound too good to be true?

This amazing sight has brought to life not only the whole world but also the very stones of Armenia.

Let us listen to them.

SONG
ABOUT
STONE

There are many different stones in Armenia, but you'll hardly find a single "illiterate" one... Just scratch the surface of any of them with your finger nail, and you are almost bound to find either a hieroglyph, or bold Armenian letters, decorations or carvings.

The Armenians call their country Hayastan — "the country of Armenians".

But there is another similar-sounding word for it — Karastan — "the country of stones". Armenia certainly is a country of stones. It is intersected by over twenty mountain ridges, and over nine hundred large and small mountain peaks. About two-thirds of the territory of present-day Armenia is covered by mountains and solid rock. And even the rest of the land, which over the centuries has been trampled by the hooves of foreign invaders, seems to have become rock-hard, too!

The fields and mountain slopes of Armenia are so rocky that it seems as if they were once covered by a stone forest, which was felled, leaving only stumps and hummocks.

According to a folk legend, when God created the Earth, He stood on the mountains of Armenia and as He sifted the huge moist mass of earth through an enormous sieve, the soft soil scattered on one side and the remaining big stone humps landed here on the territory of present-day Armenia.

The land itself seems to have been made like an enormous stone monument or statue, or more precisely, a stone monument to Armenia and the Armenian people. Later it was smashed and reduced to ruins, and the stones scattered all over Armenia are fragments of the demolished monument...

Marietta Shahinian was right to compare old Armenia to the beggar of Lermontov's well-known poem in which he was given a stone, instead of the bread he was begging for.

> "O, Country of howling stones—
> Armenia,
> Armenia!",—

Exclaimed the poet Mandelstam when he first set eyes on Armenia.

What were these stones "howling" about? After all, stones can only acquire their faculty of speech when people are struck dumb by unbearable hardships. They were howling about the hellish life of this country which, according to legend, was situated in the Biblical paradise.

They were lamenting over our people's suffering in the unending wars and invasions which exhausted our people so much that they were unable, even during the short spells of relative calm, to cultivate the land soaked in their blood because there were nothing but stones, because this was a Karastan, the land of stones!

Over the centuries the stone has been our people's curse; for centuries the Armenian peasant has "wrung" his bread out of the stone, fought singlehanded with it, subordinating it with his sweat and blood.

The volcanic lava heaped here over the centuries has created a unique "open-air" museum of stones.

Armenia is a land where one can find every type of building stone — marble, granite, bazalt, tuffa and pumice.

But, strange as it may seem, for centuries in this country abounding in stone, houses were only owned by Jesus Christ and a handful of wealthy people and the common folk lived in rough mudhuts.

Thus lived a people who had erected such architectural wonders as those at Garni, Zvartnots, Geghard, Hripsimeh, Akhtamar and Tecor. Because of the unending wars and invasions many of these architectural monuments were reduced to ruins.

There are many different stones in Armenia but you'll hardly find a single "illiterate" one. You have to walk cautiously over this land and cautiously treat every stone which appears to be rough, speckled and covered with dry moss.

You have to be cautious because if you just scratch

the surface a little with your finger nail, you are almost bound to find a drawing of a prehistoric man, hieroglyphs, Arameic, Hittite or Khaldo-Urartian cunieform inscriptions, decorations and carvings, and bold rough Armenian letters like horse-shoes which have been part of these stones for over 1600 years. They are not only "literate" stones, but also bear our signatures and belong to us.

Each of them bears the stamp of our identity, just as this land of ours bears the heavy stone-mark of our identity in the form of our architectural achievements...

In every valley and gorge and on every mountain peak there is a stone monastery, a "khachkar" (stone-cross), a bridge or a hostel, like a stone stamp reminding us that this soil belongs to us.

It was certainly not fortuitous that every enemy in turn first tried to destroy our signatures from this land, and scratch out the stamp of our identity.

Armenia! Karastan, land of stones!

Many of these stone-made monuments have been destroyed and reduced to dust as a result of the incessant wars and devastations.

The Russian tsars in the ninety years they ruled Armenia, built only a couple of military barracks and police stations out of black tuffa stones which were later destroyed by the Turkish janizaries...

With a history of thirty centuries behind them, in 1920 all our people inherited were a few buildings and monuments which had been destroyed centuries or years ago, all of which looked almost completely alike.

—58—

After the tragic events of 1915—1920 it seemed as if there weren't enough stones even in this stony country to cover the graves of the dead.

It seemed as though an old mason would soon make the last tombstone with the following inscription: "Here lies Armenia!" But that didn't happen!

Although bled white and huddled in only a very small part of their vast territory, the Armenians were at last given their *statehood* and the chance to build their homeland, and then their enthusiasm and ambitions, which had been suppressed for so many centuries, erupted like a volcano.

And not just one person, family, village or town but the entire Armenian people started building, day and night, for weeks, months, years and decades...

How long would it take to restore all that had been destroyed over the ages?

It turned out that only a few decades of new life were just enough.

Rejuvenated Armenia ordered the old stone-masons, who had been making tombstones, to build schools and maternity hospitals, and the brick-layers, who had built military barracks and prisons to build residential, clubs, libraries and universities.

Walls were being put up and covered with roofs everywhere. These walls and roofs were simple and flat at first, but there were so many of them that it seemed there wouldn't be enough stones for them. At last the stones began to serve the people but they longed for a chance to speak; they dreamed of being converted into bas-reliefs, capitals, columns, cornices, statues and memorial fountains.

They longed to become the Opera House, Governement House, Matenadaran and a Memorial to the victims of the Genocide...

The country's reconstruction went into full swing!

The inexhaustible mines of Artik tuffa stones seemed slow in providing the material so badly needed for the new buildings of Armenia.

The stones longed to speak, to find their tongue and at last they did! They invited architect Alexander Tamanian back to his homeland at a time when he was already renowned for his wonderful architectural designs in Russia.

And Tamanian became the happiest of all architects for there is surely no greater happiness for an architect then to be living in his own country when all of it is being developed.

Most of the people who used to cross the dirty, narrow streets of Yerevan in those days didn't know that the town already had its own Lenin Square, Opera House and Government House, that is, on paper...

And some didn't even notice what was happening when the tumbledown huts were demolished and foundation pits were dug for these monuments of new Yerevan. They were obviously blinded by the dust rising from the demolished houses.

What a poor old provincial town Yerevan was!

Ancient Armenian stone-carving

Here is a description by a tsarist official of the way it looked in 1882: "Houses with flat clay roofs, muddy streets and squares surrounded by clay walls... Mud, mud, mud, everywhere". I myself first saw Yerevan much later, in 1927, (although I am now rightfully considered an old Yerevanian), but I saw it almost as it had been in 1882.

The cart in which I was sitting as my family moved from Ashtarak to Yerevan crossed present-day Shahumian street, and then the centre and stopped in front of a mud house close to the present-day Moskova cinema. Crooked, narrow streets, dreary houses which seemed deeply offended by the world and to have turned their backs on the streets, high grey walls and a deadly heat and dirt and dust everywhere.

This is how Yeghisheh Charents described it:

> Yerevan...!
> An old town — calm and grapy,
> And streets — narrow, crooked, dusty...
> The time — noon-day... all seem to sleep,
> And clad in dust from head to feet...
> Then, hark... "A-ee...! "A-ee..!
> Filling the air and stretching fast
> Of a sleepy, sunken donkey...
> A blazing sun
> In a blue sky,
> And a dry air
> Too hot to breathe
> And with your streets ,
> Lost in the dust...
> That's what you are!
> Yerevan,
> Yerevan...

Donkey and carts were the main means of transport in those days.

Yerevan, then a small provincial town which began and ended with Astafian street (now Abovian), was scarcely noticeable at the bottom of a bowl surrounded by hills.

In the evenings the winds sucked so much sand and dust into the bowl of Yerevan from the barren hills around that you could only see a few yards ahead of you.

Our elders used to curse the town as they asked us children to water our yards and doorways to dampen the dust!

The town's one and only municipal clock with its expensive foreign glass-cover broken long ago had become a favourite roost of crows and sparrows which perched on its rusty hands and made the clock run fast, slow, or stop it entirely, as they wished...

Life itself stopped like the clock and it seemed as though nothing could ever change in this sleepy town which dreams of large towns and tells Charents about its longings.

.... It keeps talking,
Wants to be hanged!
— I am weary of life,— it says,—
Tired of thinking of what is bad,
Comparing me with towns mad...
Towns that glow, as brushed shoes do,
Under the light of the bright moon...

5—Seven songs about Armenia

Where the horse-carts give way to cars,
And the street-lamps shine like the stars...
Where the bridges, just like ear-rings,
Are seen hanging from iron strings...

Towns too bright, all shaped in gold,
While here I am, rotten and cold...

Charents,— it says, lend me an ear,

It is my wish to be like them...

And see to it that like a stem,

A new town is planted here...

But a few years after that, newly-born Yerevan was already making itself heard in its dusty cradle. Its clay walls and flat roofs were being pulled down and replaced everywhere by bazalt foundations, marble columns and arches. The walls of the newly-built tuffa buildings were being decorated with stone deer, and stone roses...

Many people in their lifetime had called the old architect Tamanian a romantic and even a dreamer!

They had reason to do so.

You see, in 1924, Yerevan had a total population of 30,000 and Tamanian was designing a city for 200,000!

This might well cause the inhabitants of present-day Yerevan, whose population now exceeds a million, to smile condescendingly. Yes, the unprecedented speed at which our life is progressing has turned our dreams and plans into everyday reality.

The old architect had to alter and expand the general plan of Yerevan three times! What else could he do?

Yerevan, which for centuries had been lying in a bowl of mountains, suddenly began to rise up along the sides of the mountains and then spill over the next plateau as far as Nork and Kanaker. And now it is flowing rapidly south towards the River Arax and Mount Massis and north towards Lake Sevan.

Every year the same number of houses are built in Yerevan as existed in the whole town in 1920.

The stone has begun to speak and sing!

The new buildings and monuments of Yerevan have begun to challenge the best monuments of the past and sometimes surpass them.

More buildings have been built in new Yerevan than were destroyed throughout its history; the number exceeds people's wildest dreams.

Only a few cities in the world have their own special hall-mark.

Any stranger to Yerevan at once feels he has come to the capital of a country with a unique history and style of architecture.

Yerevan is now one of the most beautiful cities of the Soviet Union and the Lenin Square is one of its most outstanding architectural monuments.

There have been many cities in Armenia in the course of its history, including legend-shrouded Ani (one of Armenia's ancient capitals) but none has or could have been built within a few decades and as finely as Yerevan.

The singing fountains in Lenin Square

The city of Yerevan, though as old as Babylon and Rome, is dear to us not so much as a forefather, or father but as a son and grandson reared by us.

You see, what we call Yerevan today — Lenin Square, the main avenue now under construction, the new residential districts in the north and south-west, each as large as old Yerevan of the 1920s, the new streets, the State Opera House, the Matenadaran and the statue of David of Sassoun — is incomparably younger then the people of the same age of Soviet Armenia and some of its districts are even younger than our children and grandchildren.

The cement on many buildings of the new residential districts on the right bank of the Hrazdan and Nork and on the new skyscrapers still smells fresh.

In 1968, we festively celebrated the 2750th anniversary of Yerevan. Our guests from all over the world drank the strong Armenian wines and the cold beers and were too busy enjoying their delicious drinks to realise that about two and a half thousand years ago the first inhabitants and guests of the fortress town of Erebuni—Yerevan had also drunk strong wine and beer in the same place.

They drank wine made from the vines which may have been planted by Noah himself and refreshing beer, which a little later the historian Xenophon tasted and described in his *Anabasis!*

And, finally, one should add that even the fish they ate might well have been the pink-speckled salmons caught in the waters which had just stilled after the great Flood.

And what about the doves? The doves, of course,

haven't changed, they had only given birth to new generations. The first was the one which Noah set free from his
Ark on the top of Mt. Ararat to see if the floods had receded and if any land lay visible.

That dove brought a green shoot back to Noah. And
now the winged hairs of the dove fly down in flocks to
the same ground to feed.

Yerevan is a very old city indeed! The old people,
aware of the dignity and splendour with which they have
been surrounded in their old age, want to live even longer.

According to one explanation of the name of Yerevan,
it was the *first* piece of land to have been seen by Noah
after the Flood had receded.

"Yerevats! Yerevats" ("It's in sight!") Noah is suppo-
sed to have joyfully exclaimed after catching sight of
this dry piece of land, thus naming our city Yerevan.

But we did not celebrate the birthday of Yerevan according to a legend or myth. We did so in accordance with
a most authentic cuneiform document!

On the 2750th anniversary of Yerevan, we had, I think,
some guests from Rome but none from Carthage, Ninveveh
or Babylon because, like others of its contemporaries, the
latter unfortunately have been reduced to ashes. But one
should remember that we celebrated the anniversary of
Yerevan not so much for its antiquity, as because it has
survived and has been given new life.

You see, as I've already said, all that we call Yerevan
today has been created by *us,* the new residents and builders of Yerevan. Now each of us is fully entitled to carve

an inscription, like King Argishti, on the walls of any building and monument of Yerevan such as this one:

"I, Gevorg,
Son of the teacher Grigor of Kond,
Built this city of tuffa,
And named it New Yerevan...!

Whereas before Yerevan expanded sideways, moving in ripple-like rings at a threatening pace towards the foothills of Mt. Ararat, it is now rising up towards the peak of Mt. Ararat!

The city already has many nine to eighteen-story buildings which in some places have screened off the view of even our most majestic monument — Mt. Ararat!

But no matter how many new tall buildings there are in Yerevan, the most characteristic features of its silhouette are the numerous bird-like cranes, the heralds of future Yerevan.

Cranes, unfinished buildings and dust, the eternal Yerevan dust which has always been here and has changed only its origin and nature...

I am afraid this dust will be hanging over Yerevan for a long time to come (the poets call it "gold dust" to placate the residents of Yerevan). There are, you see, many buldings and districts still to be pulled down and many new ones still to be built.

And so, we have to put up with the dust of building sites, cranes and unfinished buildings...

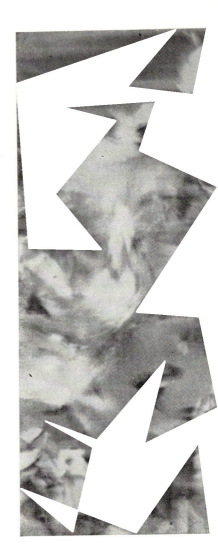

The Doves of peace

Despite this dusty confusion, the most characteristic feature of Yerevan is its warmth and homely cosiness.

This is because we have only just started putting into order our home which was demolished time and again, and tidying and furnishing our new home.

Signs of this are not only to be found in the greenery, artificial lakes, miniature monuments, small cafes, the fountain-springs, murals and sculptures, memorial stones and vast decorative vases...

Every tree and bush, every building and statue in Yerevan seems to be affectionately looked after and tended by us, like all the objects in a house by a good house-wife. They retain the warmth not only of our hands but of all the one and a half million Armenians living in exile who come to Yerevan as pilgrims from all over the world in the same way as Christians go to Jerusalem, or Moslems to Mecca.

Yerevan is only a city, but it contains, to use an eloquent Eastern turn of phrase, different towns and a thousand different types of Yerevanians, ranging from the old citizens and those who moved from Armenian villages, to the newcomers from New York, Aleppo, Marseilles, Teheran, Athens and Patras, Milan and Cairo...

Each of them is in his own way dissatisfied with Yerevan when he doesn't find what he used to see in his city; each of them sees to it that all the best things found in the place he came from are also to be found in Yerevan.

This in itself might well explain why Yerervan is becoming increasingly more beautiful and larger every day.

And how could it now grow more beautiful when for the first time in its age-old history, for over half a century now, Yerevan is being built at an unprecedented rate, instead of being destroyed and reduced to ruins!

Every five years a new district is added to Yerevan, which is almost equal in size to pre-Soviet Yerevan (the city is now twenty times larger and its population has increased several dozen times).

As for Erebuni, whose first inhabitants were the six thousand prisoners-of-war brought there from the regions of Khald and Tsubaini, there are ten times more spectators at one of the stadiums of Yerevan during a football match than there were inhabitants when King Argishti founded the fortress town.

Then there's Armenian architecture...

The spirit, character and essence of the Armenian people has perhaps never been expressed in any other field of art in such depth as in architecture...

Unfortunately, we have inherited little of our civic architecture — a few semi-ruined buildings in Ani and a few inns and bridges. So when we talk about old Armenian architecture, we mostly have in mind churches, monasteries, fortresses and the wonderful "khachkars".

If architecture is music in stone, then all these monuments are the songs of our identity, which have been turned into stone by the winds of time.

They are the most perfect expressions of our art, the diploma, as it were, of our identity, the stone carving of our people in this earth.

It is by no mere chance that way back in the early Middle Ages our architecture attained the kind of perfection which was also to leave the mark of its influence upon the architecture of other countries.

The pointed dome of the Armenian church, which under the strong 'atmospheric pressure' of foreign tyranny became rather deflated and flat here in Armenia, found refuge in Europe and freely soared upwards and, according to many outstanding art scholars, gave birth to the Gothic style!

By its very presence architecture has the power to gradually and silently instill taste. Consequently, when I first saw the renowned Gothic cathedrals of the world, I was not at all surprised because I understood that their soaring lines and forms had already been instilled in me when I was a barefooted little boy and wore out my trousers together with my school-friends on the so-called Sellan stone in the church-yard of St. Marineh in Ashtarak.

Likewise, long before learning my Armenian ABC, I had already sensed the enchanting power of perfectly harmonious architecture when I played children's games in the church-yard of the monastery of Karmravor in Ashtarak...

By the way, Ilya Ehrenburg, who had seen many architectural masterpieces during his travels across the world, was amazed by Karmravor when we visited it in 1956...

And it was only somewhat later, after studying the history of our people, that I came to understand why our

cathedrals, which had given birth to the Gothic style, could not have its splendor, enchantment and majesty not to mention the distinctions brought about by the differences in faith, of course).

You see, a splendid building would have immediately caught the eye of the foreign aggressors, who were eternally present in our history, and it would have been reduced to ruins.

Our architectural monuments could not be built magnificently because the construction of a large building requires a long period of peace-time and we only had short respites between wars...

They could not be built to look graceful and fragile because our ground was always shaking under the hooves of invading horsemen and a fragile building would not have withstood this thunder. And how could they have looked splendid in a devastated country!

Our monuments vary greatly but — just as the Armenians in exile in other countries remembered and recreated their "spiritual homeland" in their own way, they all have the same roots and their trunk and crown are always different...

The best proof of this is the Church of Geghard carved in the rocks, which is unattractive to look at (so as not to attract attention) but a marvellous work of art inside (at least for us Armenians to admire). It is not majestic, elegantly-proportioned or grandiose but it is like Armenia itself, which has deeply hidden its heavy marble beauty and secret essence...

This is also true of the seventh-century Church of Hripsimeh, a study of which will reveal the entire history of our people, its spirit and character. It is not majestic but magnificent, beautiful and severely strong without being dull.

The exceptions in the form of the three-tiered Church of Zvartnots and lavishly decorated carved exterior of the Church of Akhtamar only substantiates the cruel law of which I have spoken and which is also testified by the grave of the founder of the Armenian alphabet, Mesrop Mashtots.

Over the centuries our enemies, first and foremost, savagely destroyed everything connected with our scripts and literature.

And if in these conditions the grave of Mashtots has not been sacrileged for more than one thousand six hundred years, it is only because it was inconspicuously hidden far away from the enemy under the ground in the plain-looking cellar of an ordinary chapel, or, rather, in its foundations.

Otherwise, it would hardly have remained unscathed in the ground above where everything was destroyed.

... Our history has for the most part been a history of ruins, or a lament over ruins...

We have, for instance, rich literature on the ruins on the Church of Zvartnots, *but almost nothing on the building of Zvartnots itself!* One can easily find a mountain of books on the ruins and excavations of Ani but hardly anything on the town of Ani itself, its life, customs, arts and handicrafts, inhabitants and history.

Our history has indeed been one of ruins, losses, and past glories... And we spoke too often about our splendid glory and sacred ruins of the past, forgetting the present, walking forwards but looking backwards all the time.

... At times we forgot that we couldn't go on building our present by solely glorifying our past; that we couldn't build new monuments and memorials by praising the ruined monuments of the past.

Quoting myself to support my own ideas isn't the best way of going about it and if I put forward as evidence one of my poems written in 1947, it is only because it expresses more clearly what I have just written:

> You blind pilgrim of sacred places,
> Mind you, I love, too, memorials of old,
> They allured me, too, with all their graces,
> When still nothing new was on to behold...
>
> I do love, as well, memorials of old,
> But the only thing that makes me love most
> Is when we erect new ones fair and bold,
> In memory of those which are ruined, lost...
>
> While you dig them up, wherever you may,
> And praise the relics, amazed more and more...
> Had our forebears behaved in this way,
> Who would ever build those abbeys of yore...?

Yes, this is how it was! We visited our ruined monuments with the devotion of pilgrims and glanced at our new prosperous villages and towns on our way there as if they supplemented these stately ruins! But it should have been the other way round.

It would probably have been possible to build seven new towns like Ani if we had put all our energy into building a new instead of sighing over Ani.

The reason why I am speaking about this problem at such length and with such feeling is that fortunately it is now behind us... The ruined monuments now stand alongside fine new ones and have been put into perspective.

All their best features have been given to the new buildings and monuments of Armenia.

The ruined Church of Gagikashen has been rebuilt as the stately Opera House and the Church of Hripsimeh as Government House. The high reliefs of the Church of Akhtamar reveal to us the secrets of the two thousand-year-old history of our theatre and embellish the facade of our new theatre. The numerous "khachkars" are now miniature monuments, landmarks and memorial fountains on both sides of our highways...

You only have to see the colonnades, arches and wonderful stone carvings of our present-day Yerevan to appreciate our past history and its place in our life...

You see, even the most glorious period of the past of any people would be meaningless, if it remained only in the past. In such a case one would have to turn round to look at it, like a peacock does to admire its luxurious and beautiful tail...

What's more, the carvings on the stones of Zvartnots have become ever dearer to us because they are now used to decorate the facades of our new buildings and monuments, and the cuneiform inscription of King Argishti I has become one of the stepping-stones between the fortress of Erebuni and our present-day Yerevan...

And even Mt. Ararat has acquired greater significance since we made it our national emblem.

Only now has Yerevan, a city with a history of thirty centuries behind it, introduced itself to the world.

This splendid city of ours has a character and a national style of its own. However, the city may lose a great deal if it continues to develop in the same way.

Critics in the past were justified in saying that our shortcomings were only that we played too much on our virtues in the same way!

Anyone trying to follow national traditions of style by designing the entrance to a modern factory like the gate of an Armenian medieval monastery, would be debasing and ridiculing the very idea of national style in architecture.

If it weren't for the examples (regretably few, for the time being) of new, contemporary architecture, or rather, successful attempts to express the national form by modern means, it would daily become harder for me personally to show my home city to visitors.

In architecture, as in any other field, preserving national traditions does not necessarily mean repeating

them mechanically, but keep developing them, creating a new type of national form and quality which will express our present-day life as an integral people. It doesn't take much intelligence to realise that tuffa is more attractive than concrete.

By this I obviously do not mean that everything should be built in beautiful tuffa. It would of course be impossible to build tall appartment buildings in our contemporary towns by hand!

But are new residential districts filled with dull and faceless concrete boxes the only alternative? If this is the case, not only a drunkard, but even some-one like Sherlock Holmes would find it hard to distinguish his house from the rest!

No, we have to find a new type of national form, language and style of construction capable of harmonizing aluminium and glass, tuffa and carved stone, perfabricated panels and walls, arches and pillars and iron and concrete.

Even this small piece of land known as Armenia has had several old capitals in the past — Armavir, Artashat, Dvin and Vagharshapat but Yerevan is the best and happiest of them.

And what about the numerous villages huddling against Yerevan like a brood of chicks! The names of all of them express the hopes of several generations who were driven out of their native towns and villages or forced to escape during the Genocide: they all have been named after the towns and villages which were destroyed during the Genocide and have now been restored and snuggle round their mother-city of Yerevan — Aresh, Zeitun, Cilicia, Sebastia (Sivaz), Kharberd, Hadzen, Arabkir, Balahovit, Malatia and Nor Geghi...

But Yerevan is not the only city we cherish...

The town of Gyumri, now Leninakan, which once had seven churches and not a single three-story house, now threatens to overtake Yerevan, if Heaven forbid, the latter should ever slacken and fall behind.

And a poor old village nestling in the forest by the name of Karakilisa, now Kirovakan, has become not only one of the most beautiful towns of Armenia but its engineers and technologists, up-to-date factories and many scientific research institutes now compete with those of Yerevan.

And what about the regional centres and villages?

Churches are no longer the only stone buildings in the Armenian village. Nowadays, splendid palaces of culture and other fine edifices can be seen all over Armenia.

The Church of St. Marineh used to be the most striking building in Ashtarak. Now the town's inhabitants are trying to solve the problem of pulling down or "moving" some of the tall buildings which are screening the view of the beautiful church dome!

And what about the towns which are still waiting to be marked on the map?

Almost immediately after World War II, I visited my engineer friend Ashot Hekimian on a stony wasteland at one of the construction sites of the Gyumush Hydro-electric Station. When we pegged the first tent down, we had no idea we were founding a new Armenian town — an honour of the highest kind which in the past was only conferred upon kings and legendary heroes!

... The stones, which since time immemorial have been our curse, have now become a source of wealth.

The inhabitants of this stony land have learnt to get the best out of stones.

They are now not only used for constructing buildings, roads, fences and columns, but for making fertilizers for the soil whose cultivation they have hindered so much, and for preparing precision instruments in spacecrafts.

All our crockery is ceramic!

The crystal made from Armenian stones is not inferior even to Czech crystal, as Czech specialists themselves testify. Our stones are converted into a type of fire-proof material used to make blast-furnaces in many towns of our country.

They are used to make synthetic rubber, resins and automobile tyres.

Tuffa and pumice stones are converted into new types of concrete, heat insulators and beautiful ceramics...

Our specialists are now using the inexhaustible deposits of the so-called "hot stones" of nepheline syenites to make more than ten kinds of most valuable material, such as fine silk.

Who would ever believe that the enormous quantities

of rough stones scattered all over the fields of Armenia were not ordinary stones, but balls of fine silk!

Nowadays, it is hard to find a single stone in Armenia, be it tuffa, pumice, marble, granite, perlite, obsidian, bazalt or nepheline syenite, which is not put to some good use.

In addition to such useful minerals, as the Vardenis gold, copper from Ghapan and Alaverdi, molybdenum from Kadjaran, Agarak and Dastakert, iron from Svarants and Hrazdan, we may also mention useful "mineral" stones such as tuffa from Artik and pumice from Ani, marble and bazalt from Khor-Virap, limestone from Ararat, perlite from Aragadz and syenites from Hrazdan...

Whereas before, only bazalt and tuffa, which were mostly black, were used as building materials, now you can see tuffa stones of all colours of the rainbow in the new buildings of Armenia including violet, yellow, red, motley-coloured marbles and blue bazalt...

Unfortunately, the multi-coloured stones used for building in Armenia are heavy and their transportation is too complex and expensive. Otherwise, it would have been possible to use them in Moscow, Leningrad, Kiev, Tbilisi, and throughout the world as their deposits are inexhaustible!

Armenian tuffa, bazalt, granite, marble, pumice and perlite stones are widely used everywhere...

And we should not forget the remaining mountain ridges, rocks and rocky gorges.

The Eagle-capital at Zvartnots

The mountains of Alaverdi and Ghapan now yield seven times as much copper. The mountains of Kadjaran and Agarak are a wonderful source of molybdenum and rare metals. The whole of Yerevan is on top of an inexhaustible mine of stone-salt and Vardenis...

Well, who would have thought that it could have hidden so much gold in the depths of the earth for so long! But who was to get the treasure?— the Tartar-Mongol aggresors, or Byzantine and Turkish or Persian invaders?

The stones have not only brought our country to life, but immortalized all those who worked, fought and gave their lives for it.

Many rocks lying idly in Armenian valleys have been used to build pedestals and statues of Lenin, Shahumian, David of Sassoun, Komitas, Sayat-Nova, Nalbandian, Isahakian, Toumanian, Charents, our father-ancestor Haik, the fire-born Vahagn, Abovian, Mother-Armenia, Vardan Mamikonian, Andranik, Griboyedov, Haik Bezheshkian (Gai) and embellish the streets and parks of our new towns.

One other monument has been erected in Yerevan: a memorial to the victims of the 1915 Genocide; its eternal flame burns night and day over the Tsitsernakaberd Hill on the bank of the River Hrazdan...

The construction of this monument dragged on for long, for almost every worker had a brother, father, sister, or grandparents perished in the 1915 Genocide without a grave or tombstone.

Though abounding in stones, Armenia has often been unable to lay even a simple stone over the graves of its most cherished sons, such as Movses Khorenatsi, Khachatur Abovian, Daniel Varouzhan, Grigor Zohrap...

Even today the bones of the unknown victims of 1915, scattered all over the deserts, gorges and caves of Mesopotamia waiting for a tomb of their own, glow white in the day-light, and emit dull phosphorus light at night...

The construction of the memorial to the victims of the Genocide went too slowly because each of the builders was building, as it were, a tombstone for his dear ones, and would often stop work to remember those appalling days...

It was built slowly but firmly and forever because it had to be both a memorial-sepulchre and a monument to the renaissance and miraculous resurrection of our country and people...

After kneeling reverently before the eternal flame over the tomb of the victims of the Genocide, you come out from the stone dome, which seems about to collapse, and you find yourself viewing the most important part of that monument — the panorama of our new flourishing Yerevan spreading around the Tsitsernakaberd Hill which, more than any other architectural "device", symbolizes the renaissance of our people...

Innumerable Armenian stones have been used for the Grave of the Unknown Soldier and for the embellishment of the memorial fountains immortalizing the memory of the heroes who lost their lives in World War

II... Their glory is as durable as the stones and as eternal as the water flowing out of the memorial fountains...

Let us stop in front of one of them and remember the immortal Armenian heroes, and following the flowing stream, let's listen to a new song...

SONG
ABOUT
WATER

This country of mountain rivers would have most probably died of thirst, if the greatest of all rivers — that of History — had not changed its course...

This was true for many centuries until quite recently...

Twenty or thirty years ago a train passenger on his way from Yerevan to Moscow would notice that within a few miles of Yerevan all the greenery vanished and he would be rolling through a desert stretching right up to the valley of Lori — a desert first glowing salt-white and gradually becoming dark-red.

Desert was a typical landsape in old Armenia. After centuries of invasions and massacres its soil was either sodden with bitter tears, whose salt had turned it white, or irrigated by blood, which had turned it dark-brownish, like clotted blood.

It was precisely here, in the desert of Sardarapat, that in 1918, the "remnants" of our people, who had somehow managed to escape death during the Genocide, worked one of the miralces in the history of Armenia. With every rusty implement they could get hold of, such as spades, axes and hoes, they halted the march of the invading Turkish hordes, the allies of the Prussian warmongers, and conquered a handful of land in their own native country for a handful of orphans and refugees...

These were indeed hard and hopeless times...

The Russian troops had withdrawn from the Caucasian front. Enfeebled by civil war, Soviet Russia had been forced by Germany to sign the shameful Treaty of Brest and then the Germans had violated this treaty and invaded the Ukraine. In the Caucasus the Turkish assassins and their allies created havoc. It seemed as though the Armenian people, abandoned by all their allies, would give way under that enormous war machine which had torn our people apart and left them bleeding white after the Genocide.

The total destruction of Armenia seemed so imminent that Vehib Pasha sent a telegram from Sardarapat to the Turkish rulers informing them of his impending success in erasing the name of Armenia off the map of the world for ever!

But then one of the most characteristic features of our history once again made itself apparent. A handful of our people, who had survived, realised their existence and that of their homeland were at stake and came out in force,

Lake Sevan

mustering their last ounces of strength, and started *a patriotic war,* in the full sense of the word, a struggle of life and death. And they proved once more that it was impossible to annihilate a people and that a people could work miracles in any situation which seemed utterly hopeless.

So that's what the desert of Sardarapat means to us!

It was here indeed that the freedom war
Of new Avarair was battled again..
It swept over us like a monstrous roar,
Yet forced Mher[1] not out of his den...:
We no longer had the brave prodigies...
As Vardan[2], Yeghisheh and Ghevont Yerets[3],—
But a hell of mess —
        orphans, refugees,
The battle itself —
        with heroic deaths...
And the brave were born out of that woe,
And the dim hope flashed with a fierce thunder,
And even Allah,
        let alone the foe,
Would have shrunk in fear in sight of this wonder...
The soil bore the brunt of the deadly fight,
And was crushed to death in its every part,

---

[1] Mher — a hero of the pouplar epic, *the Dare-Devils of Sassoun.*

[2] Vardan Mamikonian — the Armenian army commander in the national-liberation Battle of Avarair against Persian troops (5th c.A.D.).

[3] Yeghisheh and Ghevont Yerets — instigators and chroniclers of this Battle.

And tears and black blood shed there overnight,
Left us this desert of Sardarapat...

All the bells of the village churches on the Ararat plane tolled day and night, sounding the alarm and calling the Armenian people to the battlefield. And the Armenian people were quick to respond. Men and women, the old and young kept coming with whatever weapon they could get hold of — rifles, sickles, spades, stones, and sometimes armed solely with their teeth...

Most of them knew that they were confronting instant death and their detachments were thus known as "shroud-bearers".

Before going into a critical battle the Armenian generals and troops used to go to Etchmiadzin and kiss the right hand of the Catholicos of All Armenians and ask for his blessings.

Contrary to tradition, this time the Catholicos himself came to Sardarapat to tearfully kiss the rough mud-smeared hands of the Armenian peasant soldiers joining the decisive battle...

And then a miracle occurred.

The Armenian people, although bleeding white, halted the march of the Turkish hordes.

The invasion of Armenia and total annihilation of the Armenian people were not the sole aims of the Turkish invaders. They hurried towards Baku, trying to join forces with the Germans, to seize the oil of Baku as soon as possible and strike a final blow at the Baku Commune and the newly-founded State of Soviet Russia.

And although the invaders reached Baku, according to the chief of the German Staff General Von Ludendorf, they failed to seize the Baku oil "because of those cursed Armenians". At the end of 1918 they were forced to capitulate.

At the Battle of Sardarapat our people not only won the right to exist but risked their lives to save the Baku Commune and newly-born Soviet Russia.

... Even today when one looks out of a train window at the last scraps of the stony desert, one can't help wondering if this country had really no water at all.

But this question seems quite meaningless when one arrives in the Lori Valley and hears the joyous babbling of the mountain stream of Devbed, remembers the blue rippling waves of Lake Sevan, or the roaring falls of Shaki, the rumbling of the Hrazdan and Vorotan rivers and the gentle murmur of the River Arax...

There was water. At least, there was enough water for our small land.

But the mountain streams gushed downwards, passing our parched soil by and heading towards the great rivers, steppes and seas.

My friend Rassul Hamzatov was right in saying:

> You crazy waters of mountain streams,
> Look how the soil cracks in the torrid heat,
> While you keep rushing to the steppes and seas,
> To pour your waters which they wouldn't need...

And you keep flowing, babbling merrily,
Leaving us for good, far from your land...
While I find myself robbed of every glee,
When I have to leave for a foreign land...

... Mountain rivers are sometimes violent and turbid and ours were especially so because of their anger and sorrow...

It is not easy to leave one's own homeland for good without contributing to its progress in some way or another!

But how could they be of any use when on their short way out of the country they had to flow through gorges which were too deep and as far from the soil, as the earth is from the sky...?

And even if the water of a stream was in someway extracted, it was used at the most to irrigate the meagre orchards and vegetable gardens close to the banks of the river or provide just enough power to turn the millstones...

Just as the rain bypassed the parched fields and poured down into the sea, so over the centuries the river water roaring with anger, only dug deeper and deeper river-beds, laying bare the roots of the willow-trees which turned yellow.

The mountain streams flowed violently, letting the fields and orchards and the soil a few feet away from their banks erode and crack.

There was plenty of water flowing through the gorges but only a few feet away it was worth its weight in gold!

The rocky shores of Lake Sevan

It is not fortuitous that water in this country has been worshipped since time immemorial...

The legendary water of Katnaghbyur is said to have stirred Tsovinar, the heroine-mother of our epos, *Sasna Tsrer,* (The Dare-Devils of Sassoun) to conceive and give birth to the epic heroes Sanassar and Baghdassar...

Water has always been praised and revered in Armenian folk songs...

The common folk in Armenia still sing the famous medieval song in verse — *The Youth and the Water,* which is an ode to water and sounds like the babbling of a translucent stream. Here it is:

> The water flowed down the hill,
> Ran through the field and out of it...
> A playful youth came with a thrill,
> To wash his hands and face and feet...
> He washed in joy and loud scream,
> And overjoyed he asked the stream:
> — From which hill-top are you flowing,
> My gentle stream, crystal glowing?
> — From the mount, there, far beyond,
> Bearing the snows, both fresh and old,
> — To which brooklet do you proceed,
> My gentle spring, sweet and placid?
> — I go down to those brooklets,
> Feeding flowers and violets...
> — To which orchard are you speeding
> My sweet and cold, refreshing spring?
> — To that orchard where I can see.
> The old gardener waiting for me...
> — And to which spring you go to meet,

My gentle stream, glassy and sweet?
— I go to join that water-spring,
Where your darling comes up to drink...
Oh, let me stick my lips to it,
And have my love with hers replete...

This is not only a song in praise of life-giving water, nor a lament over love as pure as spring water, but the secret cherished dream of a worker to become the owner of his land.

Among the witnesses of the age-old cult of water are the famous Armenian pagan goddess Nar or Nurin (who is still revered in most Armenian villages), the enormous stone dragons (*Vishaps*) scattered at the foot-hills of Mt. Aragadz, and the castles, which were built at the source of rivers just to guard the water!

But the stone dragons scattered along the river were powerless against the dragon-like foreign invaders...

They were supposedly guarding the source of the river, while down below in the valleys and fields people were fighting for a drop of water and irrigating their cornfields and orchards with their blood, sweat and tears...

In the Kotaik region a stone with the following inscription carved on it has been preserved: "This water belongs to Agamanants Melik. A curse on whoever attempts to use it!"

Anyone visiting the cemetery of Ashtarak can still see a gravestone whose inscription explains that the man buried under it was killed by his neighbour in a quarrel over water!

The stone is as dry as the soil of Armenia and covered with moss, which does not even bear the name of the deceased, but explains the most important things—roughly why and where the poor old villager was killed.

How can one explain what a *water-stone* is to children who are always playing by the beautiful fountains of Yerevan and spraying water over each other by plugging the water hole with their fingers?

A *water stone* was a large tuffa bowl, shaped like a church dome turned upside down and supported by wooden poles. In the early morning it was filled with murky water from a river or a brook, the water was filtered and then used by the people as drinking water.

The dirty water dripped drop by drop into a pail or a clay jug, set before it. You had to have the patience of a saint to collect a little water and quench your thirst on a hot day.

And a wise old man sitting in a smoky room would spin yet another tale about what would have happened to this country and its people who were dying of thirst if the greatest river, that of History, had not changed its course and the dragon sitting at its source had not been killed!

As soon as the last volleys of war in Armenia had stopped, the Armenians began digging their first water canals. Since then hardly a year passes without a new canal being dug in Armenia. Among them are the canals of Etchmiadzin, Hoktemberian, Shirak, Garni, Sisian, Talin, Kotaik, Arzni — Shamiram, to name but a few...

Just as one can't count the number of blood-vessels in one's body, neither can one count the large and small canals, pumping stations and irrigation systems which have been built in Armenia over the past decades.

They include older canals such as the Shamiram and the Ashtarak canals. Many centuries ago these were used to irrigate the lands of the Urartian kings but now they have been turned into canals to irrigate the common lands of Ashtartk and Etchmiadzin, day and night.

In his famous letter Lenin was indeed right when he advised us to give priority to the problem of water and irrigation — the most vital one facing us in those hard early years. And Nansen, the great scientist and Armenophile, who was invited to Armenia for the opening of the Shirak canal, declared that the very people who were on the brink of total annihilation were now watering the green tree of their rejuvenation!

Is there any need to explain to an Armenian peasant, worker, or intellectual of peasant stock what a new canal and water mean to a land which had been dying of thirst for so many centuries?

Armenian grapes and other fruits are said to be especially delicious because the soil, which used to be so bitter, is for the first time being irrigated with water instead of blood and is now giving us all its sweetness which bas been a secret for centuries.

I believe this is true and swear that everything in this land is just as sweet!

Why is this so? Because everything has been squeezed

out of this soil, I mean out of these stones, with a great deal of sweat!

But water does not only mean cornfields, new orchards, gardens and memorial fountains...

The people of Sassoun, who lived among the stony crags of Mt. Aragats, are now being allocated beautiful stone houses along the banks of the Talin canal.

The reason why they chose to live in the high mountains is to be found in our age-old history of wars and invasions.

It is quite understandable that the Armenian peasant, who for centuries had been attacked and ravagely plundered, sought shelter and built fortress-like villages in the impregnable mountain peaks.

The village of Megri, a comparatively small one, is, for example, surrounded by four fortresses built on high mountain peaks. As intended, they defended the village up to 1920, when they were converted into "historical monuments".

So, for the first time in its history, the Armenian village is being moved through choice and not because it is again in danger of being burnt down and the people of being massacred. The move is accompanied by the sounds of the *Zurna* (an oboe-like instrument), hooting car horns and energetic dancing.

So, for the first time in Armenian history, villagers voluntarily are leaving their village, bidding farewell to the mossy tombstones of their ancestors and moving to villages where there are no tombstones as yet, but many newly-born babies...

Armenia has a severe and cruel climate, and nothing at all will grow here without water, unlike in Georgia and Moldavia. A villager from these republics may come back home in the evening, accidently leave his walking stick by the wall of his house and in the morinig find that green shoots have sprouted from it, so fertile and mild is the soil and air there!

You may go to any region of Armenia, Ashtarak, for instance, and from some distance you can at once make out the borders between the irrigated and non-irrigated land, the border between life and death, where the greenery ends.

Talin is a wild stony area. It is like an enormous unsown field, which every year produces a splendid crop of stones!

And the stones of Talin, which had "run to seed", grew in number yearly because there was nobody to combat them...

And why should they fight for? Even if all the stones were crushed and sifted through an enormous sieve and turned into earth, the most vital thing of all would still be lacking — water.

Now the waters of the new Arzni-Shamiram canal have reached the wild stony areas of Ashtarak and Talin and the people there are waging a real "Patriotic war" against the stones to save their land from domination.

Before long, the stony areas of Talin and Ashtarak will be covered with greenery and the inhabitants of the poor old mountain villages will move into beautiful houses...

The people of Sassoun will come down from the mountains to live in these new villages, too. They will settle in the plane, retaining at the same time memories in their hearts of their eternal Sassoun and their mountain spirit:

Whereas the people of Sassoun are moving down into the valleys, the residents of most of the villages of Zangezour, including Khntsoresk, are climbing upwards or to be more precise, they are emerging out of the abyss of human history when people still lived in caves.

And one of the reasons for their move is again water.

They used to have no reason to leave their primitive villages as they knew only too well that all they would find would be parched deserts. Besides, poverty is poverty everywhere — in the mountains and in the valleys. And it doesn't matter where people live if there's no water.

But water does not only mean vineyards and orchards, cornfields and pastures. Today it means, first of all, energy, light and all the power which gives a country life, from small industrial workshops to powerful electronic accelerators!

Today it's hard to find a single "idle" river in Armenia. They are all used by large and small power stations, which give our country millions of kilowatt hours of electro-energy. The River Hrazdan alone now has six hydroelectric stations in the short distance between Lake Sevan and Yerevan.

The light in a club of one of our mountain villages went out recently during a concert. One can imagine the chaos that followed and how the audience cursed the poor electrician while he mended the fault! These villagers, who a couple of decades ago had lived for centuries in darkness, or at best under the light of an oil lamp, now could not bear to be in the dark for a few minutes!

Light has entered the life of every Armenian town, residential area, village, hamlet, mountain and valley. Armenia today has been so flooded with light that one would hardly need a map to mark its frontiers with Iran and Turkey at night — the frontier is where the light ends.

It is said, as I have written in my book *The Lights of Yerevan,* that the people on the other side of the River Arax in Western Armenia watch the lights of Yerevan every night as if they were the Northern lights or the luring rays of the rising sun, and in some villages they have become the subject of songs and tales.

The source of most of the lights of Armenia is Lake Sevan, one of the most beautiful and highest lakes in the world.

This lake, one of the inimitable wonders of nature, is so high up that at times it is hard to make out whether it is a cloud gliding over the lake, or blue waves dancing in the sky... It is indeed a unique wonder of nature and it seems wrong to make practical use of it, but...

At this point one should be reminded that in the thirties *the only source of light and irrigation in our poor country was Lake Sevan* and like a mother, it sacrificed its beauty

—123—

and strength to save its only perishing son — Hayastan — Armenia!

Beautiful Lake Sevan and its cascading waters (Yerevan is only seventy kilometres away, but about a thousand metres lower) used to turn the turbines of six powerful hydro-electric stations, giving strength to enfeebled Armenia. But it began to shrink and expose its lime-coat sides which had always been under water.

From losing its beauty, the lake is now wrapped, as it were, in a white veil of mourning.

Most probably, unlike many of us, Sevan itself knows, that the sacrifice it has made was not in vain, and as Pushkin put it, "his sorrow was translucent".

O, Sevan, Sevan!

Magnanimous and kind, you have remained as pure and bright as a mother's heart. Forgive us if we have done you harm.

But what else could we do when only the stars and gods drank out of your bowl under the heavens and your sons were dying of thirst like the rocks on your shores?

We could only turn our thoughts to beauty a short while ago after our country had satisfied her needs for her "daily bread" and gained energy. The whole of Armenia is now striving to save Sevan's beauty and stop it from shrinking anymore.

After powerful thermo-electric stations run on natural gas have been built in Yerevan. Hrazdan, Kirovakan and other places, Lake Sevan will be given a chance to rest after all its long selfless work.

But is it possible to turn back the wheel of time and bring back the water already consumed once and for all?

A miracle of this sort may be workad if the water is 'transfused'.

For centuries the Arpa river has flowed among the snowy peaks of the Gegham moutain-ridge. Scientists have carried out research on its water to determine whether it is a suitable "donor" for Lake Sevan.

You see, Lake Sevan is a regal lake inhabited by a variety of trout known as the "prince of fish" ("Ishkhana-tsuk" in Armenian).

A fifty-metre-high dam has been built on the River Arpa near the *Jermuk* health resort. The resort is already provided with a large artificial lake and the waters of the Arpa flow into Lake Sevan through a deep tunnel, forty-eight kilometres long.

About 270 million cubic metres of water will be pumped into Lake Sevan every year, so that at least its present beauty is retained.

And so at last the arguments between the "scientists" and "artists" — the engineers and poets — will cease.

Aware of the wrong we have done Lake Sevan, we are especially anxious about it today.

The shores of Sevan are being made more attractive, trees are being planted, and holiday rest-homes, children's summer camps, cafes and beaches are being built. The most up-to-date hydrofoils are now racing across the blue waters of Lake Sevan out of which only recently our archeologists excavated a number of Urartian royal chariots were about 3000 years old!

There isn't a single poet who wouldn't praise the unique beauty of Lake Sevan after seeing it just once. But I was most struck by the poem of my friend, the Avar poet Rassul Hamzatov, about Sevan because it was Rassul's distant forefathers who two hundred years ago pillaged the wonderful monasteries on the Island of Sevan and threw many of our priceless medieval manuscripts into the lake.

> I love Massis like an Armenian,
> I share its grief like an Armenian...!

But this is all by the way.

So as not to burden Lake Sevan anymore, use was made of River Vorotan, which until recently was simply dashing idly against the rocks, and of Armenia's longest river — the Arax. As the latter marks our frontier line, we think of it more as a sword dividing our homeland in two than of the water giving it life.

In recent years we have successfully used underground waters for irrigation purposes. When used rationally, they may provide the soil with more water than Lake Sevan! Even the thawing snow is being used.

The reservoirs in Aparan, Mantash, Marnoot, Sarnakhbyur and other places are now gathering all the waters of the thawing snows and in summer when every drop of water counts so much, they are used to irrigate the orchards and vineyards of the Ararat valley.

Perhaps someday in the future when we see a stream or brook flowing across a plane, we won't find it easy to answer the question posed by the song: "Which mountain are you flowing from? "but we will be able to answer the question: "Which orchard are you flowing to?" for every drop of water.

However, even if we could use all the water available in Armenia with maximum efficiency (including the dew on the flowers), it would still be far from enough to meet the country's constantly growing needs.

The point is that we are now annually producing about three billion kilowatt-hours of energy which is obviously not enough. And in the very near future we will need 35 billion kilowatt-hours! Where will we get this amount from, if our water supplies are already becoming scarce?

The situation may be saved by natural gas which we get from Azerbaijan, Daghestan and Iran. The thermal power stations operated by natual gas are now several times as powerful as the hydro-electric ones.

The Yerevan thermal power plant alone provides the country with as much electric energy all the year round as all the hydro-electric stations of the Sevan Cascades put together. The new Hrazdan thermal-power station, the largest in the republic, has a capacity of 1,200,000 kilowatts which exceeds that of all other power stations in Armenia.

And if in the future all these fail to meet our needs,

then the atom, the good old atom, will come to our assistance.

The first atomic power station in Armenia with a capacity of 840,000 kilowatts has already been built in the Ararat valley.

Now there is certainly no town or village, mountain slope or gorge in Armenia which does not have its own water-spring...

But how many of them ever had drinking water? Even a comparatively wealthy village like Ashtarak had no drinking water for a long time and every day the children were made to fetch spring water from a nearby gorge. The young girls of other villages didn't want to marry the lads from the mountain village of Gndevaz because their married life was hell; all the daughters-in-law of the village had to walk three hours every day to fetch water from a spring in a remote gully. Even the inhabitants of Yerevan for centuries used gutter water — the first water main only came into being a few decades ago. Water in Armenia is still precious but there are now even more valuable kinds of water. Armenia has over three hundred mineral springs. Among them *Jermuk* and *Arzni* are as good as the best curative waters in the world.

At this point it would be appropriate to say something about Jermuk and oil.

In Armenia there are rivers or rather, torrents of warm, delicious curative "jermuk" which are used to no purpose. If a trifling part of the enormous amount of money spent on oil prospecting in Armenia were used to bottle and sell these valuable mineral waters, the profit gained from them would be several times greater than the income received from oil. You see, one shouldn't forget that a litre of *Jermuk* costs twice as much as kerosene. I do not mean we should stop searching for oil in Armenia. We know that nothing in Armenia is easily found and this also applies to oil. For centuries foreign invaders pillaged everything they could get their hands on and so our land was forced to hide its treasures as deeply as possible.

Water was precious in Armenia and has been sanctified for centuries as such. As a result, our people like to build fountains in memory of such places and people who are ever dear to them.

The spring-water in the Stepanavan mountain-pass marks the place where Pushkin saw the corpse of Griboyedov; the Sardarapat spring is in memory of the heroes of the Battle of Sardarapat; the spring of Gndevaz is in memory of the heroes of the Civil war; the spring of Kharberd is in memory of the victims of the Genocide of 1915; and many memorial springs have been dug in memory of all the people who lost their lives in World War II.

One old stone-mason from Kirovakan erected four springs in memory of his four sons who were killed in the War...

It is a beautiful, wise tradition symbolizing the immor-

9—Seven songs about Armenia

Water was precious in Armenia
and has been sanctified for
centuries...

tal memory of the fallen heroes with the sweet and somewhat sad murmuring of pure spring water.

The murmur of such water is dearer than gold in the torrid heat of Armenia and anyone who drinks it, instinctively blesses both those who dug the spring and those in whose memory it was dug.

These springs have greatly helped the development of miniature architecture and sculpture in Armenia. At present in many remote villages of Armenia one can come across a great variety of stone monuments which at first seem unattractive but are really wonderful pieces of architecture.

Here is one of them:

Good old fellow, just stop a bit,
When passing by these water springs...
Every village you may visit,
In Armenia's mountain-rings,

You will find them bubbling ever,
As do the songs of my country...
Bow gently in solemn prayer,
And lend an ear to our history...

Just hear the voice that comes and goes,
That stirs the hearts under its stress...
'Tis the sound of those heroes,
Who used to come to drink and bless...

Who fought their War with might and pledge,
Far from their land, and spared no strings

In stopping foes to sacrelege
The lucid source of our springs!

Now drink it, sit and rejoice,
Under the tree... The water flows,
And you may hear the sacred voice
Of the fallen warriors — heroes.

Who, as they did in time of war,
Either sadly,
              or in a bliss,—
Keep repeating the prayer of yore:
"God, give the Earth a lasting peace...!"

Quite recently a new original memorial spring appeared in one of the Yerevan parks in memory of the great 18th century poet Sayat Nova.

The translucent jet of spring water gurgles from a white marble wall on which the poet's proud face is carved, and the water seems to be incessantly repeating Sayat Nova's brilliant words:

Not all may taste the water I drink,—
    A special kind of spring is mine;
Not all may read the words I write,—
    A special kind of print is mine;
The ground I stand is not of sand,—
    Of special rock and lime is mine..!

All the rivers and lakes, waterfalls and springs, rivulets and brooks of Armenia have been put at the service of man. And they have thus become purer and clearer. They even seem to flow faster.

They are in a hurry, as if fully aware how much is still to be done; how many fields and orchards await them and how much land is still parched.

Let's follow the babbling water to the fields, orchards, and the parched land, and listen to a new song.

SONG
ABOUT
THE SOIL

Whereas "native soil" is a common expression in all countries and in every language, in Armenia it may only be used figuratively. It would be truer to use the expression "native stone"!

Spring usualy comes only once a year, but in Armenia it may be seen several times.

The mountains have their own spring, and so do the valleys and what's more at different times of the year.

Armenia is small but varied. In this handful of land one may find all kinds of climatic zones — alpine meadows and vine-yards, forests and subtropical vegetation.

When autumn comes to the Ararat valley, the grapes are succulent and the rosy peaches are ready for picking; nearer to the foot-hills of mountains it is still summer and the wheat is only just beginning to turn gold. Meanwhile, in the alpine meadows the grass is growing lushly and the poppies are in full bloom. Higher still, the snow is only just beginning to melt and the snowdrops and violets have just appeared. And the mountain peaks are always adorned with snow.

At the same time in Megri Gorge, one will find pomegranates, figs and apricots ripening among the scorching rocks.

A mountain stream flowing from the thawing snows on the slopes of Mt. Aragats will cross all four seasons of the year in the same day on its way to River Hrazdan.

There are places in Armenia which don't even see all the four seasons, but only two of them — winter and spring.

As soon as the snow melts the flowers begin to blossom and the grass shoots up before the ground has time to get warm and the foliage to bloom, the snow falls again and the small cycle is completed.

But the effect of these climatic differences was only clearly to be seen in the fertile parts of the land. The remaining land was baked by the sun in summer, swept away by the rain in autumn, and covered with snow in winter. Wild absinth sometimes grew here which helped on to discern the seasons. One sometimes also comes across lilac and yellow flowers which never faded but which only testified to the land's barrenness and poverty.

Poverty and barrenness in a country whose industrious people managed somehow to earn their daily bread from stone! And it seemed that there was no other alternative

for this country, which for centuries had only been pillaged and irrigated with blood and tears, and that nothing could grow in it except thistles and bitter absinth.

And the wind-blown seeds and fruit-stones, which sometimes took root, turned into bushes and trees.

But these trees were sickly and bent and grew scantily. You see, so as to beg a drop of rain from the merciless sky, they had to endure a great deal of hardship.

I suddenly remembered these trees when I was in the United States.

Near San Francisco there is an old redwood forest of rare sequoias. They are preserved with the utmost care and are reverently visited by many tourists visiting America.

They look more like rockets piercing the skies on their way to the stars.

Most of them are two or three thousand years old and have witnessed everything from the Roman empire, the foundation of Erebuni, Christ's birth and the discovery of America. They heard the voice of George Washington, and the whistle of the bullet that killed John Kennedy.

They are 30 to 40 metres high (the same height as a 10-15 storey building) and their trunks can only just be encircled by ten people.

They are beautiful, inspiring, proud and ambitious. Nothing can hinder their growth. Everything surrounding them — the air, sun, water and soil are favourable to them.

Like a genius, deep in thought, who forgetting about

everything else as he strives to achieve a sacred and difficult goal, so the sequoias strive to soar higher and higher, without wanting to waste time on branching outwards. No sooner have the upper branches begun to grow stronger, than the lower ones wither and drop off, so as not to burden the tree or waste the energy essential for its growth.

I looked at the soaring crowns of these giants and remembered our mutilated, wrinkled, and at times crooked and scorched trees

And it suddenly struck me that although the seeds are very important, the soil in which the seeds are planted is no less so. Ideally, the soil should be soft, moist and blessed by sun and water — the complete opposite of the stony and harsh soil in old Armenia with its merciless skies and constant lack of water.

But, however harsh and merciless the soil in Armenia may have been, it could not match the stubborn and industrious nature of the people living there.

But what could they do if the roots of poverty could only be cured by water which was nowhere to be found?

The lack of water wasn't our only problem, however. We only had a scrap of land which was covered with stones, making it inaccessible and practically useless.

Suffice it to say that even today only 15 per cent of Armenia's over-all territory of 29,800 square kilometres is being used!

The vineyards of my home village, Ashtarak, are surrounded by many small rocky hills. As a native of

Ashtarak and a peasant's son, I thought for a long time that these were natural hills and only recently I discovered that these were countless stones, which had been collected and heaped there one by one by my grandfathers and forefathers to clear the ground for a vineyard.

The vineyards of Megri Gorge are also surrounded by rocky hillocks, but here, on the contrary, not the hills but the terraced vineyards encircling the slopes and rising up like amphitheatre are man-made.

The local peasants built their terraced vineyards on the stony hill slopes and covered them with a thick layer of soft soil which they brought from a long way away. Then they irrigated them, filled with water they had fetched from the deep gorge and cultivated their amazing orchards and vineyards...

This is all they had to do to earn their daily bread from the stone. Whereas 'native soil' is a common expression in all countries, and in every language, in Armenia it may only be used figuratively. It would be truer to use the expression 'native stone'.

How long have my people suffered because of the soil! How much blood and tears they have shed for the natural right for the land to belong to them! The right to earn their bread from the land with the sweat of their brows and to build their own homes!

One does not have to be a famous archeologist and excavate ancient towns and fortresses to understand the history of this small piece of land, these stones. All one has to do is dig the earth in any part of Armenia, and one will learn the sad story of this people.

The English historian and journalist Emile Dylon described the Armenians as being a people ready to sacrifice themselves for the sake of peace, an amazingly optimistic people in situations when anybody else would be in a state of utter despair. The best sons of the Armenian people, he said, are of the substance of which history creates its heroes and martyrs.

The upper layer of our soil consists of blazing-hot copper-coloured stones and rocks — almost melted stones, which have turned into glass and scorched earth, which has turned into cement. These help scientists today to reveal the secrets of making cement, glass, silicates and other fire-proof materials.

If you uproot the absinth and weed and remove all the stones from a patch of land, you get down to a layer of soil which is heavily salted and white from the peasants' tears shed on it.

Dig a little deeper and you'll find a layer of soil which is moist from peasants' sweat. This layer is as scanty as the hope of the Armenian peasants who earned their bread from it...

Deeper down there is a thick layer of tuffa which is as red as the blood spilled so copiously by our people only recently. Next comes a stratus of black tuffa. This is the blood shed by our people in the distant past which has coagulated and turned black to mourn the past...

Below this there is a layer of blue bazalt, which is

10—Seven songs about Armenia

everywhere and, like our people's will and faith, has been hardened under foreign domination.

It is no wonder at all that this soil and the stones are dearly loved by us and irreplaceable as they contain all our life, our blood, sweat and tears and our death — the ashes of our dear ones, the ashes of the best sons of our people who have made the soil sacred.

How many times our land has saved us, empowering us with the necessary strength to face any danger and any tyrants starting with the legendary Bel to Sultan Hamid who was known to the world as the "Bloodthirsty Sultan".

This wonderful quality of our native soil was described by Pavstos Byuzand, a 4th century Armenian historian in his renowned story about the Armenian King Arshak and the Persian tyrant Shapuh. The latter lured Arshak to see him in his tent with the aim of finding out his secret thoughts and intentions. They talked and strolled around the tent, half of which, on the secret advice of Persian wisemen, was laid with earth brought from Armenia. On the "Persian side", King Arshak spoke quietly and humbly but no sooner did he tread on the soil brought from Armenia then he became proud and independent.

This native soil of Armenia, a country which was supposedly situated in the Garden of Eden but destined from the start to have a history worse than that of Hell. And how could it be otherwise when this small country lay between the powerful kingdoms of the East and West at the crossroads of the world trade routes and was therefore always at the mercy of all invaders?

The Armenian highlands, stretching from Lake Van to Lake Sevan and from the River Hrazdan to the Euphrates, not only guaranteed the domination of the most important trade routes of the Ancient World, but also held a most powerful position in military terms against neighbouring countries. This must surely explain why, from the very beginning of its history, Armenia became the bone of contention between the great powers of the world. The result was that our country was under constant attack and its people were either killed or sent into exile.

Assyria, Urartu, Rome, Byzantium, Persia, the Arabs and Seljuks, the Mongols and Turks fought against Armenia and among one another on her land.

And this land of ours has been struck by so many stormy invasions that everything in it had been converted into ruins — literally everything, except Mount Ararat which the enemies could not destroy and so took prisoner.

Apart from having a cursed history, it was also doomed to have a cursed geography. The tragedy of a people who were forced to build houses on the banks of flooding rivers or on volcano craters.

You see, Armenia is not only a land of earthquakes, cold and hot lava, and extinct volcanos, it is also the epicentre of many national and social volcanos and earthquakes and historical underground tectonic forces which have savagely moulded this land and its history.

How many times have the best sons of our people, prematurely old through worrying about the innumerable unfathomable problems involved in a peaceful and free existence, been prepared to make the most incredible sacrifices to solve this situation. They thought of taking the people away from this hellish arena of history where throughout time countless tragedies had been acted out against the unchanging background of Mount Ararat.

But who could ever imagine leaving one's motherland in search of another of calling a foreign land one's own? A homeland, which is your own self and contains your blood and tears and every part of which is imprinted with the signature of your people and sealed with its blood!

And the new cradle of your son is as much your homeland as are your ancestors' graves. One may still feel himself Armenian without the sacred white domes of Ararat but one could never feel at home! So, in spite of all their hardships, our people stayed in this land, suffered, perished, emigrated, returned and emigrated again but the land remained ours! And those who were forced to leave for good and found themselves a "paradise" to live in, have always pined for their "hellish" home and dreamed of returning to it.

"Longing" is perhaps the most characteristic word in the rich and inexhaustible Armenian language and if there is a sickness which can truly be called Armenian it is that of longing.

I don't know what people in other countries take with

them when setting out on a long journey — an Armenian traveller always takes a pouchful of soil with him. If he is leaving Armenia for good, he takes a handful of soil for himself. If he is leaving for a short time, he takes this pouchful of Armenian soil for his relatives or friends abroad.

I'm amazed how the small amount of soil lying amidst the stones, does not disappear altogether for this very reason. After all, even today thousands of Armenian refugees visiting Armenia always take away a handful of soil which they consider theirs.

This bag of Armenian soil is a most cherished keepsake for every Armenian refugee. It is kept in the most sacred place of the house next to the rusty key with which he or his ancestors locked the door of their house for the last time in 1915 before being driven into exile...

This handful of soil is sprinkled by the Armenian refugees over the coffin of their dead relatives to bury them symbolically in their native soil and for the same reason they call their cemeteries in far-off America or Australia "Ararat", "Van", or "Oshakan".

They cherish the handful of soil of their country dreaming of the day when all Armenians will be able to return there and the entire family will gather under one roof.

Just imagine what Armenia would have been like today if all the Armenians scattered about the world could have devoted their talent and knowledge to Armenia. And if they could have built here everything they have built in every other part of the world...! Just imagine what even this

...One can say that grains of wheat were found during the excavations of the Urartian fortress-towns...

barren, rocky soil would now be like if the Armenians had not exported their talents and skills abroad for centuries getting only suffering and disaster in return.

We frequently talk about something being brought into life only recently in Armenia. This is only partly true. We had almost everything in the past too, not here, in this land of ours, but abroad and for the benefit of other people.

The most important innovation today is that we are all building a new homeland in this country. This is a hard task requiring great effort and much time. After all, even today only a third of six million Armenians live in Soviet Armenia, which is itself only one tenth of our real home land. The Armenian people includes those living in Armenia, plus all the Armenians living beyond its borders and in Armenia. Armenian culture and arts include all the treasures that have been created in Armenia plus those created by the Armenians dispersed all over the world. For instance, William Saroyan, who was forced to leave Armenia during its blackest days, cannot be considered a Turkish writer, and Charles Aznavour, although he lives in France, is an Armenian by birth.

Indeed, for the first time since the fall of the last Armenian Cilician kingdom in the 14th century, we have created a new State and turned this land into a home for all Armenians.

And it is perhaps for this reason that everything now taking place in Armenia acquires a special meaning and symbolic significance. You see, the stones being converted into silk thread are the same ones which for centuries

have been our curse; the new gardens were once deserts which were irrigated only by our tears and blood; the new houses are replacing the countless ones which were destroyed and are only now standing firmly in their native land.

This land may be proud of the fact that it has never tried to occupy another land and that an innocent drop of blood has never been shed in it.

Armenia may be small in size but it is great as far as the talents and skills of its people are concerned. Their love for other peoples and everything that is kind, noble and good is truly self-effacing.

We're a small people, very small, indeed,
As small as a stone which splits suddenly,
From a mountain crack and falls madly down,
Gathering the force of a powerful rock lying in the field...!

Small,
Just as our rivers,
Storing their huge force
For those massive ones
Which flow lazily down through the field!

We're a small people.
That's all very true...
But then, who told you
To lay yourselves out
To squeeze us so much
And make us... as dire
As a priceless pearl...?

Who urged you to strike,
And strew us like stars,

So as to watch us,
Wherever we are...?

We are small! Just like
The land we live in,
The borders of which,
Stretch from Byurakan straight up to the Moon,
And from Lusavan up to Urartu...!

We are small! As small
As that wonder stuff — the Uranium is,
Which for ages long
Would glitter,
And shine,
But would never shrink...!

Who could ever say where grapes or wheat grain first originated?

But one can at least say that grains of wheat and grape pips were found during the excavations of the Urartian fortress-towns near Yerevan, which were built over three thousand years ago! What's more the grape pips were of the same varieties as those cultivated in Armenia today!

That means our ancestors sowed wheat and cultivated grapes on this soil thousands of years ago!

They, too, struggled against the stone and at the same time had to defend their orchards and fields from foreign invaders.

They struggled single-handed against the stones, cultivated wheat and barley and astonished foreigners in the 5th century B.C. with a "strange" beverage brewed

from barley known to us as beer. They turned the stones into grapes and drank delicious wine which inspired them to carve grapes and pomegranates, wheat and eagles on the stones. But grapes most of all!

Could any other symbol be dearer to our people than the vine?

You see, like our stubborn and enduring people, the vine can tolerate heat (which even makes it sweeter) and survive severe frosts, as the wild vines growing on the slopes of Mt. Hadis show.

The wine made from them is both bitter and sweet, like the fate of our people: bitter like the sufferings and privations endured by them in the past, and sweet like their hope and faith in the future...

It is not fortuitous that the vine, like our people, has withstood numerous invasions and wars over the centuries and survived to this day.

In 1919 only five thousand hectares of vineyards were left in Armenia.

Five thousand hectares of ragged, wrinkled roots, the fruit and leaves of which had been burnt by fire and trampled under the hoofs of invading horsemen!

It looked as if the last vine would be uprooted like our ancient people.

It looked as if somewhere an old vine-grower would toast the last glass of wine squeezed from the last cluster of grapes to the eternal peace of Armenia's soul;

But this was not to be.

The Armenian vine-growers and sowers, who had taken

Our land is small but there's always plenty of room for guests....

up arms against the last Turkish hordes, returned to their vineyards and fields and set to work again!

All they found was a few trampled ears of wheat and a charred vine with only one cluster of grapes!

Their immediate task was to restore the broken ears of wheat and cultivate the charred vine, but at that time the national emblem of our new Armenia was being created and they decided first to imprint these ears of wheat and cluster of grapes on the emblem next to the hammer and sickle.

It would be impossible to imagine finding a higher honour for the vine than that of symbolizing our people.

This symbol thus became the object of a concern of the entire people and acquired national significance.

From that day on hardly a year passes without new vineyards being planted in Armenia!

The vine is hardy and stubborn, but it likes gentle treatment and attention and in return gives its sweetness as a reward to man's labour.

It is not for nothing that its roots and branches look like a peasant's rough, wrinkled hands.

The vine, as it were, always stretches out its hand-like branch in search of support as it rises upwards. Its roots are deep but it is modest and sprawls along the earth, but if supported, it can rise upwards.

And rise it did!

The fields and gorges of the Ararat valley turned into green lakes and rivers of vineyards...

These rivers soon reached the foot-hills and now the

vineyards "reside" not only in the Ararat Valley, but also in Noyemberian, Shamshadin and Talin and their varieties, which withstand the cold, have already taken root at a base on Lake Sevan and in the Ashtarak regions.

The vine gradually conquered almost all the reasonably fertile parts of the Ararat valley, covering Yeghvard, all the wildernesses on both sides of the Yerevan-Ashtarak highway and was only halted by the soil paved in stone in the Talin and Ashtarak regions.

It would have stood still for a long time if the waters of the Arzni-Shamiram canal had not reached it.

As you remember! *"In the begining God created the heaven and the earth; and the earth was without form and void..."*

These words from the Bible seem to have been referring to the stony fields of Ashtarak and Talin. For six thousand years nobody had ever touched this unfinished part of the world created by God!

And it was only recently that the suntanned vinegrowers of Ashtarak and Talin, equipped with tractors and other machines, completed the Maker's work.

As someone who has witnessed it from the start, I must say the vinegrowers' task was most difficult.

Imagine an enormous desert "paved" with smooth stones where only weeds grow in the handful of soil carried by the wind into the cracks between the stones!

The heat is so intense that the air hovers before your eyes like a transparent curtain and you cannot tell whether a

11—Seven songs about Armenia

black swarm of midges is circling in the air, or black spots are flashing before your eyes.

They are most likely black spots because the heat is so intense that nothing living stirs and even the snakes are roasted and blackened by the sun, and the poisonous tarantulas, glittering here and there, do not dare to come out from under the stones.

It really does seem as if God has just created this wild chaos and left it unfinished to attend to some more important matter.

But then suddenly one hears the roar of an engine which is most startling in such a barren place.

The stone-picking machine drags its enormous hook over the stones, suddenly finds a crack between them, sinks its hook deep into the crack and with a loud roar the machine pulls out a huge rock, turns it over and drops it on one side. Then it does the same with other stones.

At times, in spite of its great efforts, the machine scrapes only thirty or forty metres of rock and then stops! That means the area of rock is too large and only dynamite would help.

But exploding the stones, turning them over and removing the wildly-wriggling balls of snakes from under them is only the start of the work.

Tractors must be used to remove first the big rocks, then the smaller ones or rather the stones as large as mill-stones, and then people must collect the smallest ones, turn the soil underneath, smooth it, and only then can it be irrigated and a new vineyard planted.

All this is done in the blazing heat amidst the tremendous noise of machines and in the thick dust whipped up by the very strong wind which settles on everything — even the words spoken aloud!

This stony desert is so impregnable that a special vehicle base has been set up to develop it. However, in spite of the impressive variety of equipment, the work is so hard that the development of each hectare costs 750 roubles.

To understand the enormity of the work being carried out on our land, suffice it to say that Ashtarak, which for centuries has been famous for its vineyards had only 1300 hectares of vineyards before the Akanates canal was constructed in 1960. When this barren land is fully developed it will have 16000 hectares!

The only consolation for this hard and highly expensive work is that the soil has gained strength with time and the hot sun is very good for the sorts of grapes from which excellent brandy is made.

It is said that in the distant past this stony land around Ashtarak was used as a shooting-range! But then every part of Armenia was in fact a shooting-range and had seen fire and destruction since the very beginning of our hard history until a few years ago.

And it is highly significant that the shooting range is being converted into a vineyard, that the soil scorched by

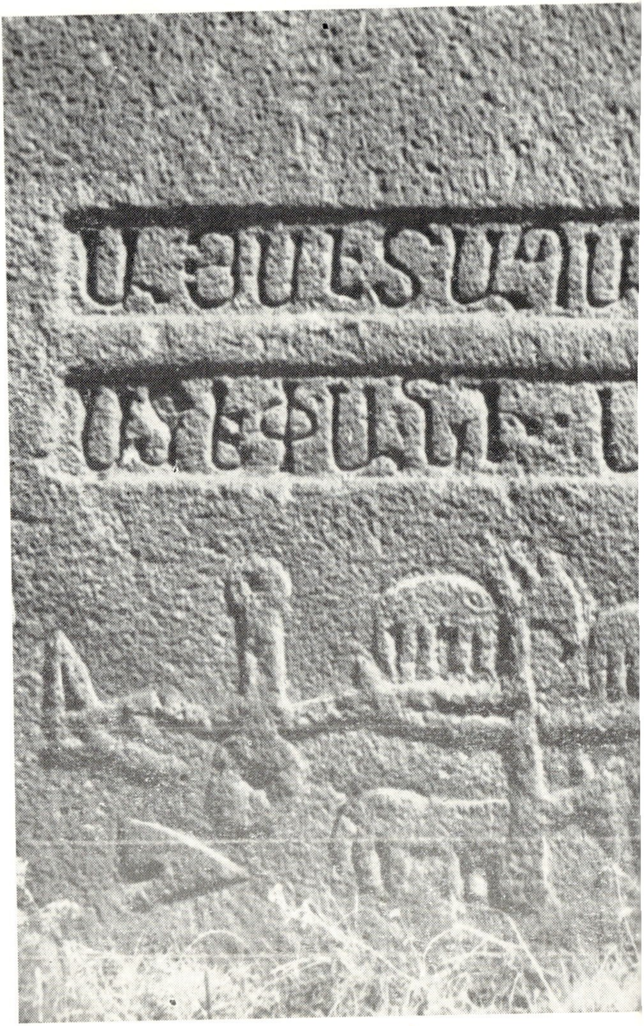

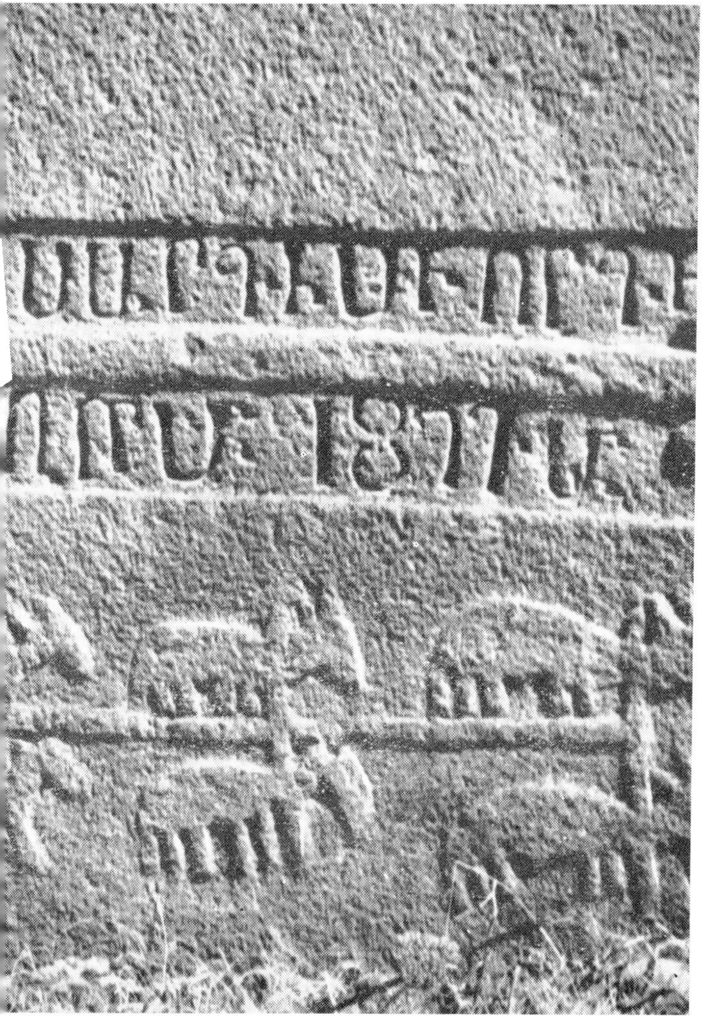

the fire of centuries-old wars is now being clothed with a green mantle of peace!

The virgin lands, however, are not only being converted into vineyards. In the former barren lands of the Ashtarak region, which have now been converted into vineyards, seven new residential districts have come into being, each with 1000—1500 hectares of vineyards! That means hundreds of new families, weddings and babies!

... Our land is small but there's always plenty of room for guests and anyone visiting our homes to share our hospitality, wisdom and experience.

Our vines are small but can fill an endless number of friendly glasses of sparking wine and brandy. In just one year the old barrels of the *Ararat Trust* are filled with eighty million litres of wine and six million litres of brandy!

So there's enough for one cup for each of us and the rest is for you! Just help yourselves, friends of Armenia, wherever you may be! Raise your glasses and let us toast our home...

Our land has revived and so have our agricultural workers. The misfortunate peasants have now got rid of mud-huts, soot, dung, bast shoes and the bitter smell of poverty which hovered over this soil for centuries.

In his new stone-house the peasant now has a bathroom, a gas stove, a radio and television, book-case and refrigerator, his children's school certificates and diplomas and a car in a garage outside his house.

For his hard labour on the land he has been given

awards; he has visited the Urals, Moscow, Sofia and Kanzas state; his picture has been printed in newspapers, at agricultural and even art exhibitions!

At home he listens to the radio broadcasts from his village, concerts from Yerevan, songs from remote India and space rocket signals; on T.V. he watches men landing on the Moon, football matches played in London, documentaries on sunny Italy and skating competitions in Grenoble!

In the village club or Palace of Culture he meets and listens to famous Armenian writers and sometimes foreign writers and artists. He sometimes goes by car to watch a football match or go to the theatre in town and spends his summer holdiay by the sea.

And if today the village youth, who enjoy an incomparatively better standard of living, are dissatisfied and try as hard as they can to move to the town, it is partly because they are no longer illiterate peasants cut off from the rest of the world. They want film-festivals, Brazilian football, literary discussions and ballet on ice!

... I will never forget that memorable day when our family moved from Ashtarak to Yerevan in a horse-cart. As soon as we crossed the old stone bridge of Ashtarak, we saw a few yellow patches of arid fields, beyond which the desert extended as far as the gardens of Yerevan.

Moss-covered scorched rocks, parched earth, wild absinth, dilapidated ruins and then Black Makich's Gorges, Robbers' Gorge and Ransack Gorge...

In the darkness the black stones looked first like wild

beasts and then like people. Both were dangerous, but men more so, for nearby was Robbers' Gorge.

And what was most frightening was that when you got closer to the rocks, they no longer seemed like people at all. A person, even a robber, was better then this oppressive feeling of desolation.

"This is how I shall die — barefooted on the road", complained my old Aunt Asanet who often made this journey on foot (she seemed old to me, although she was only forty at the time!).

And the poor old woman did, in fact, die without seeing Ashtarak jump over the river Kasakh and reach the cross-road of Yeghvard, then sprawl halfway along the Ashtarak-Yerevan highway, filling the space between them with murmuring water, new vineyards and settlements which soon united and made the lonely road into the busy Ashtarak Avenue of Yerevan.

By the way, Etchmiadzin, Artashat and Arzni have merged with Yerevan in the same way. It would be a good idea, if the planners and builders of the Yerevan Underground took into consideration and built the Metro Stations of Yerevan-Ashtarak, Yerevan-Artashat, Yerevan-Etchmiadzin and Yerevan-Abovian straightaway because they became suburbs of Yerevan long ago.

My Aunt Asanet died without seeing how Ezras, one of the numerous orphans put in the Ashtarak orphanage after the Genocide (whom my Aunt often treated to nuts and wild olives) went to Moscow to study and became

Our land has revived and has
our agricultural workers.

the famous scientist Ezras Hasratian, one of Academician Pavlov's closest assistants.

She died without seeing one of the new districts on the Ashtarak-Yerevan highway which bears the name of her neighbour's son — a mischievous lad who used to destroy birds' nests, and later became the outstanding scientist and cosmologist Norair Sisakian...!

But enough of that...

Sounds of folk instruments are coming from the orchards of Ashtarak, inviting us to at least one of the seven wedding feasts in full swing in Ashtarak...

The wine harvest is at its peak in the vineyards. Whenever you look. you see grapes; whatever you touch, you feel sticky grape juice...

The juice boils under the sun, ferments and there is so much steam from the fermenting juice that you feel drunk even without tasting it!

Music is playing, the young wine is fermenting, and the flames from the meat roasting on the spit are sparkling. Vehicles are taking the grapes (day and night) to the wine and brandy factories...

Let's follow one of them to the factories of Armenia. There are lots of them and they're all different. And let's listen to a new song...

SONG
ABOUT
FIRE

Yes, our land was born of fire, though for centuries the fire has done little good- in furnaces, hearths and foundries- but plenty of evil in wars and conflagrations...

Heaven was in pains!
The Earth was in pains,
And the purple Sea was also in pains!
And amidst the sea labouring to bear,
Was the crimson reed...
Out of the reed-pipe
Ascended smoke...!
Out of the reed-pipe
Ascended flame...!
And amidst the flames
Ran a youthful blond,
With his hair of fire,
With his beard of flame,
And with both his eyes
Just as real as suns...!

This is how one of our old
folk songs describes the birth
of Armenia amidst fire and
flames.

Armenians are not idol-worshippers, but they venerate fire, as it symbolizes their homes and hearths which were always in danger...

Whenever the Seljuk warriors wanted to find out the nationality of their prisoners, they ordered them to sit by the fire. They knew that whoever at once started rearranging the burning wood and adding branches to increase the flames was Armenian.

A blazing hearth, smoke wafting gently upwards from the chimney—what more did the Armenian peasant or the country need to be happy?

But what could the fire of a small hearth do?

Could it ever enlighten the whole country, or at least consume and destroy the rags of the country's age-old poverty?

Armenia emerged from fire and flames; but for centuries fire has done little good but plenty of evil in wars and conflagrations...

True, in the remote past metal was cast at Metsamor and the Urartians mined gold in Zod but this became simply a historical fact long ago.

The fires of the numerous modern factories of Armenia are brand new; they were lit by the crimson sparks out of which like our legendary Vahagn, our new Armenia, was born.

And, what's more, it is thanks to these new fires that Armenia, which · formerly used to import only wars and disasters and export orphans and refugees, now delivers unique precision instruments not only to many distant parts of the world, but also to space.

We used to compare our achievements to those before 1920. Nowadays that would be simply ridiculous. You see, it's one thing to say that something has doubled or trebled in size, but quite another when it has become five or six hundred times larger.

Besides, such a comparison is altogether impossible because a lot of old things simply didn't exist in the past.

A leather factory, Ter-Avetikov's artel, the Shustov and Sarajov wine factories, and a few small workshops — that was all Yerevan had in the way of industry in the past.

Whereas our soil, stones, water, literature and songs have existed for centuries and have now been given a new lease of life, there was no industry at all forty centuries ago, or even forty years ago (except the primitive copper mines in Ghapan and Alaverdi).

True, there were big industrialists, bankers and oil tycoons but they lived and developed their businesses outside Armenia in large towns and industrial centres such as St. Petersburg, Moscow, Paris, Constantinople, Tbilisi, Baku, Cairo and Rostov.

All the big plants of Armenia were built in the 1930s and 1940s, and for the most part after World War II.

In 1828, Yerevan had seven churches, six inns, 51 water mills and a few of primitive workshops. Even in 1890, all the real estates in Yerevan (including the industrial ones) amounted to 281,000 roubles.

That means any of our present-day collective farms could easily have bought all of old Yerevan and paid mortgages on other towns, too.

When you see the largest modern factories of our present day Armenia and the vast army of the skilled Armenian engineers and builders, you can hardly believe that the first water-main in Yerevan took sixty years to build, and in 1912 specialists were invited from Germany to build the first horsedrawn tram!

Incidentally, in 1912 Yerevan enjoyed a comparatively prosperous period and the town had already grown so rich that the annual output of its factories and workshops totalled 84,000 roubles!

To appreciate the "enormity" of this sum, one only has to be reminded that just *one* of the factories of our present day Yerevan produces several hundred thousand roubles' worth of products *daily!*

But we have strayed from the subject again. It is too early to talk about the hundreds of thousands when we are still standing amidst a crowd on the Kanaker Plateau, watching the 11th Red Army enter Yerevan...

That was on December 2, 1920.

The red banner of October waved in Armenia. The banner was now there, but there was still no Armenia. There were only ruins, ashes, a dark-blue smoky sky which gradually brightened, and stones everywhere like fragments of a destroyed memorial to Armenia.

Where should one begin? How could a new country and a new life be built on these heaps of ash and stone?

Other countries have fertile land, coal, oil, forests, sea or prosperous towns. Armenia had literally nothing except grey stones and blue sky.

There was no way out: a new Armenia had to be created out of these stones and sky.

And so that's what we did!

First, we gathered the limestones scattered in the fields and with the tenacity of alchemists, turned them into carbon!

Then, we combined nitrogen with the carbon and made fertilizers for the soil. After that, things went more smoothly.

In a word, our people, newly-risen, like poor Lazarus and endowed with creative strength, called out: "Let there be Armenia!",— and Armenia was born.

Then, continuing our creative work, we turned the carbon into rubber and the rubber into tyres.

The new industry of new Armenia was founded on the day the workers of the Ivanovo region presented Armenian workers with some of their weaving-looms for the foundation of a textile factory in Armenia.

The oldest of these looms, which was pensioned off long ago, may now be seen in one of the exhibit halls of the Yerevan Museum of Revolution.

One of Armenia's first factories was founded with these looms — the textile factory of Leninakan.

It was soon followed by others: Yesabov's small enterprise was converted into a canning factory and the Lepse workshop into a machine-building factory.

Since then many huge factories have been built in Armenia but none of them have aroused so much joy as the first small ones.

But then things started happening. Frightened by the noise coming from the construction site of the Dzora Power Station, the wild deer and birds of the Lori Gorge fled to safety. The dust in the forests of Kirovakan was soon mixed with the gold-flecked (but unfortunately, poisonous) smoke of the chemical plants. And Armenia, which had no experience of manufacturing rubber, became an important production centre of synthetic rubber

Yerevan, which used only to be famous for its wine, cognac and dust, in the '30s began producing carbon, chromic iron, glass, mullite and machinery.

The Ghapan copper mines began producing several times more copper for the needs of the newly-born Armenia, the new copper-melting works in Alaverdi produced not only copper but also the traditions of the new Armenian working class.

And then the war began...

During the hard war-years building wasn't interrupted for a single day.

It was during those ominous years that the huge edifices of a machine-building plant sprang up near the slopes of Mt. Ararat, the rubber in Yerevan was converted into tyres and cables, the merry chimes of the first clocks produced in Yerevan began ringing out and the chimneys of the aluminium plant towered high in the sky on the Arabkir Plateau...

New plants were put into operation and the old ones improved and enlarged.

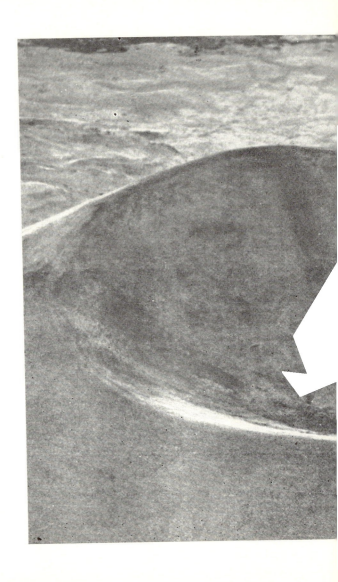

The walls around the Kirovakan Chemical Works had to be pulled down three times during the reconstruction work.

I saw fragments of the first two walls and the third wall around a superb workshop of artificial rubies which any highly developed country might be proud of!

For centuries Armenia has been known as an agricultural country, a country of shepherds and their songs.

The main character of a book, its reader and frequently its author were countrybred and their taste left its mark on our literature. The theme of industry, which has existed for only a few decades in Armenia, still lacks flesh and blood and hasn't yet entered literature.

And this is evidently why there are factories everywhere in present-day Armenia except in books (with a few exceptions).

Not only the absence of traditions is making itself felt but the fact that only what is old and time-hallowed is considered "poetic" and "national" in character.

Even now some of our writers believe that a shepherd (or an elderly man) in a "papakha" (sheepskin hat) speaking in his particular dialect is a truly "poetic" and "national" theme, whereas, say, a young scientist making an electronic computer, or listening to Charles Aznavour is not.

And they do so at a time when it is as hard to find a shepherd in a sheepskin hat in Armenia today as it is an illiterate worker. No wonder young people with good secondary educations readily come to work at our modern factories!

If you go round the shops of these factories, you will see that many of them are just like the laboratories in scientific research institutes. Everything is perfectly clean and tidy, and the workers are in white overalls.

Such enterprises are only twenty years old. But we are already receiving reports on their products from countries as far off as India.

Could the illiterate Armenian peasant of the past, who was even afraid of airplanes, ever have dreamed that the electric equipment made by his sons and grandsons would be used to give electricity to villages in far-off Vietnam, or be sent to the Moon and Venus?

And the fact that Armenia is "involved" in all this, may be proved not only by the Armenian instruments used up to now in spacecrafts, but by the "Orion 1" and "Orion 2" space observatories, launched recently, which were both made in Armenia.

Today Armenia supplies even highly-developed industrial countries with several types of most sophisticated and complex machinery.

One hundred and fifty types of industrial products made in Armenia are exported abroad to many European and Asian countries.

These Armenian products include super-precision measuring instruments, watches, synchronic generators, synthetic and plastic materials, lazers, various types of lathes, Nairit rubber and Hrazdan and Nairi computers.

Many Czech specialists know nothing about the country of Armenia or Nairi but all of them know about Nairit rubber.

Very few German physicists and mathematicians have been to Armenia and seen the small Hrazdan river but many of them have made calculations with the help of a Hrazdan and Nairi computer, which were highly praised at the International Leipzig Exhibition.

Whereas Armenia used only to export raw materials and half-finished products, and until quite recently, only rare machines and high-precision instruments, it has now begun exporting whole factories! Engineers from the Yerevan Electric-Machine-Building Plant have designed and built a similar plant in Baghdad.

Only a few years ago the first Armenian car was made at one of the new factories in Yerevan and it was called "Yeraz" ("dream" in Armenian).

Well, of course, one can understand how proud people here were of this first Armenian car. But I think they overstepped the mark by giving it that name.

But in fact, it can be explained much more easily: the word is simply an abbreviation of three Russian words "Yerevanskii Avto-Zavod" (Yerevan Automibile Works).

In the same way, "Arus", an abbreviation for "Armyanskii Uskoritel" (Armenian Accelerator), the enormous electronic accelerator in Yerevan is also a lovely Armenian feminine name!

And all this is taking place in our Armenia, the smallest of all the republics of the Soviet Union, which is, however, in 3rd to 5th place as far as the production of the most important varieties of industrial products in the USSR is concerned: electric machine-building, machine-tool building, instrument making and chemical industries, etc.

One should be reminded that Armenia covers only 0,13% of the territory of the USSR, and its population represents 0.9%. It isn't surprising, therefore, that in Armenian folk-tales the youngest brother is always clever. And it's quite understandable why Indonesian specialists find it hard to believe that Armenia, a country supplying them with sophisticated machines and precision instruments, is only slightly larger than their island of Bali.

How simple and easy it used to be to write about Armenia's factories, which produced only such commonplace things as wine, tinned food, honey and even rubber, which then was already a familiar product.

Now, however, it is hard enough to remember correctly, let alone write about the products of the new factories. Take po-li-vi-nyl-ace-tat, for instance!

These words sound strange and mysterious and their products are frequently difficult to examine and sample, unlike brandy, for instance. That is surely why most people simply do not believe that the production of at least one of these enigmatic "acetates" is several times more profitable to Armenia than the famous Armenian brandies.

Armenia has long been known as a country of cont-

rasts, a country of highly-developed culture and poor rural life...

For centuries Narekatsi's manuscripts and Aristotle's translations existed along with Armenia's smoky ceilings and stoves, heaps of dung, ploughs, poverty and illiteracy. For centuries Armenia was endowed with a powerful spirit but a feeble body, so to speak.

It is only now in our life-time that this powerful spirit is gaining just as powerful and healthy a body. Whereas Armenia used to be advanced exclusively in the arts, it is now making progress in industry, technology, astrophysics, radio-electronics, and space research.

Armenia is becoming a huge scientific research institute and laboratory where many complex problems of the twentieth-century science and technology are being investigated and solved.

One of the best proofs of this is the electronic accelerator which was recently built in Yerevan.

When, in 1961, the rocks on a lonely spot by the River Hrazdan were blasted to make way for the accelerator, who would have thought that specialists were not only blasting rocks but also the nuclei of atoms and electrons?

This huge machine is the most complex and sophisticated structure ever built in Armenia although it was called by the lovely tender woman's name "Arus"! (Incidentally, this original idea has become a tradition in the scientific world: since then almost all the world's powerful accelerators built in America, Germany and elsewhere have been given women's names!).

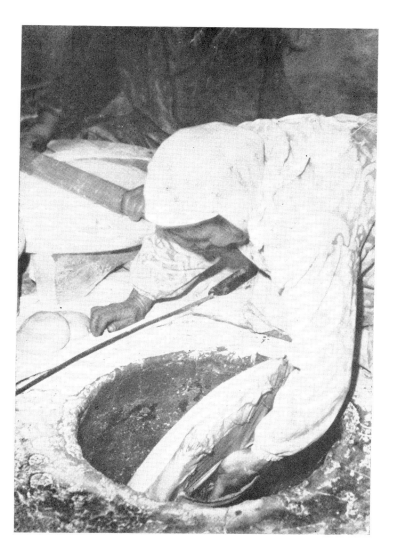

An Institute of Physics, a Research Station of Cosmic Rays, an Atomic Power Station, an Electronic Accelerator, a Laboratory of Space Astronomy.

This surely means that Armenia also is slowly being converted into one of the developed centres of theoretical physics.

But I've so far only spoken about the past and present. You can imagine what the near future will be like when you know the sum of money invested in developing industry and science over each of the next ten years is to be many times more than that of all the past decades together.

In just the last five years, the industrial output of Yerevan has grown five times in size and amounted to two billion roubles in 1970, compared with 84,000 in 1912.

It would take many pages just to enumerate the factories built and being in Armenia in recent years. And since they are mostly being built in towns, it follows that now 60—70% of Armenia's population lives in towns.

The result of the natural growth of the population, the repatriation of Armenians living abroad and industrial construction is that small Armenia is at present one of the most densely populated Soviet republics.

The latest data show that there are 93 people per square kilometre in Armenia today. The figure is undoubtedly much higher for Yerevan!

But in spite of this, the hardest problem now facing Yerevan is finding the necessary manpower, even now that young people are pouring into the towns as they cannot find jobs in their villages because of the mechanization of agriculture.

For this reason, factories, which until recently were being built only in towns, and mostly in Yerevan, are now being built everywhere and will be so in the future. Thus, many of the regional centres and villages of Armenia are turning into towns and comfortably-designed villages.

A huge complex of copper-molybdenum plants has recently been opened in Agarak. At the southern border of Armenia, on a formerly deserted rocky area a marvellous town with a small population and subtropical climate has appeared. It's name has not been put on the map yet.

And that is not surprising at all since even Hrazdan, a future centre of the chemical industry is still not on the maps of the USSR! Hrazdan, a holiday resort which arose next to a large complex of mining-chemical enterprises!

It is worth saying a few words about the people who built this complex.

During World War I an orphan by the name of Manvel Manvelian escaped with other orphans and refugees from the ravaged town of Van and fled to Eastern Armenia.

After losing all his friends on the journey, the boy got to Yerevan with great difficulty. Armenia, which was then as poor as him, gave him bread, a pencil, an exercise book and an alphabet learner.

The little boy first began selling cold water in the streets and avenues of hot Yerevan and then became an apprentice to a dyer. He began writing poetry at school,

—193—

trying in words to express his gratitude to his homeland which had saved him from death.

But it seemed as if fate had decided to give him other means of expressing these feelings.

Soon the young boy became engrossed in chemistry and subsequently became one of the most eminent chemists of Armenia.

During World War II a vast aluminium plant was built in Yerevan which was to operate on the raw material brought from the far off Urals.

This fact, typical of our recent past, was not very logical and alarmed many people. And it was perhaps for this reason that the chemists of Armenia began searching feverishly for valuable raw material in Armenia itself.

Manvelian knew that in other places, for instance, in Volkhov, the alumina used as the basic raw material to produce aluminium, was obtained not from bauxites, but from nepheline syenites, whose deposits were practically inexhaustible in Armenia. But the trouble was that the alumina would cost a great deal and besides, they would only be using the alumina, potash and cement, and all the remaining valuable substances would be wasted. But there was no other way out: the aluminium plant in Yerevan was already in operation and Armenia didn't have any bauxites.

And the young chemist began his long and complex experiments to obtain alumina by a new method from the nepheline syenites, knowing that his success would open up large perspectives for Armenia's national economy. In this

perfected method of obtaining alumina, the nepheline syenites are treated thoroughly without any valuable substances being lost.

Thus, besides the alumina, one can now obtain valuable substances such as the metasilicate of calcium and natrium, *yerevanits,* white dust, Portland cement, potash, etc.

In a word, this means the mining-chemical enterprises being built in Hrazdan, besides their basic product — alumina — will provide the country yearly with one and a half million tons of cement, white glass, washing and whitening materials, fine crystal and flint soil of the highest quality which is indispensible for optical glasses and semi-conductors...

Over ten substances, which are highly valuable for the national economy, are to be obtained from ordinary stones, whose deposits are practically inexhaustible in our country. This is indeed the most eloquent "poem" dedicated to his homeland by Manvelian, who never became a poet...

Incidentally, the words "poetry" and "chemistry" don't sound at all strange together...

Since time immemorial all of Armenia's life has been imbibed with the love of learning and education. Examples of this may be seen everywhere today, including in our chemical plants.

I recently visited the Yerevan Aluminium Plant on business and I was amazed by everything I saw there.

In front of the factory's building, instead of dull concrete columns and discoloured boards, one finds the wonderful statue of the eagle of Zvartnots.*

On the building's facade, instead of slogans written on a piece of cloth left over from the last celebrations, one sees Yeghishe Charents' lyrical lines on the revival of our country in sparkling aluminium letters.

On the walls of many of the shops one sees the portraits of our outstanding writers, artists and scientists.

Even the ordinary work shifts are named after popular heroes, such as Grigor Narekatsi, Hovhannes Toumanian, Yeghisheh Cahrents shift, etc.

This fine tradition was started by the former director of the Aluminium Plant, one of the best known chemists of Armenia, the late Abet Dovlatian, and according to many of the factory workers, it greatly helps to increase the workers' enthusiasm at work.

Armenia has changed beyond all recognition.

Huge plants and enterprises are being built in almost every part of Armenia, except, I think, in Idjevan. Mind you, only recently a new large carpet plant has been built there. After all, Idjevan is the northen gate of Armenia, the threshold of our paternal home and we, Armenians, have retained the custom of laying carpets under the feet of guests entering the house.

This is what the factories of Armenia tell us about. This is what has taken place in this land of ours in a few

---

* The eagle of Zvartnots — a copy of the eagle from the capital of the ruined Church of Zvartnots.

Panorama of Yerevan at night...

decades! All this sounds like a miracle, but it's a miracle which may be explained.

The innumerable hardships, constant strain and resistance against evil, the amazing talent of finding a way-out of any seemingly helpless solution, have sharpened people's wits and kindled their desire to build and create, which has been repressed for centuries. And when ways of doing so are found, the people can indeed work miracles...

If a people, encircled by packs of human wolves for so many centuries, could do so much all alone, just imagine the things they are able to do now that their powerful skill is erupting like a volcano...

Finally, if the old saying "two heads are better than one" is true, then just think of the vast united skill and intelligence of the fraternal nations of the Soviet Union which makes each of them doubly more powerful.

If today numerous Armenian experts are working in every part of the Soviet Union, many skilled experts and scientists, workers and builders from all parts of the Soviet Union are working here, in Armenia, too.

It would have been utterly impossible to produce electronic computer machines in Yerevan without the help of scientists and experts from Moscow, or find and use natural gas in Armenia without the help and experience of Bashkiria, Turkmenia and Azerbaijan, or complete the most complex construction of the underground tunnels of Arpa-Sevan without the generous assistance of Ukrainian and Byelorussian builders. The same is true of the production of the "Yeraz" automobiles without the advice and experience of experts from Riga and Lvov; and the mounting and roofing of the electronic accelerator without the skill and talent of experts from Leningrad.

Isn't this what has helped the output of industrial products of Armenia to increase so much that in one day we now produce the same amount as we did during the whole year of 1913?

Our present-day Armenia is so powerful that it seems to have "absorbed" several hundred old Armenias! It can now afford to take care of its exile sons scattered over hundreds of countries all over the world.

It is by the command of revived Armenia that every year Armenians, who miraculously survived the Genocide, return to their ancient homeland.

They come back like the pages of a book entitled *The History of Armenia* which were scattered by a storm.

Let's leaf through this book and try to unfathom the secret of this people's tenacity and longevity.

Let's listen to a new song, a song about letters. .

SONG
ABOUT
LETTERS

For one thousand six hundred years the letters of the Armenian alphabet have defended the national identity of our people, like a regiment of thirty-six courageous soldiers...

Tormented for centuries by wars and disasters, our people would hardly have survived until now unless they had owned, along with the sword, a most powerful weapon — a written language.

Whenever they were unable to triumph with the *sword,* they triumphed with their letters, destroying their enemies, and passing down their hopes, faith and dreams to future generations.

In spite of innumerable disasters, over twenty five thousand Armenian manuscripts have been miraculously saved. And they not only help us unfathom the secrets of our people's legendary endurance and longevity, but, as Valery Bryusov so wisely said, are "testimonials to the nobility of the Armenian people".

These manuscripts contain most valuable information not only on Armenia, but also on the history and culture of many countries and peoples of the ancient world, since this land of ours, one of the first cradles of mankind and its culture, was the cross-road of the fate and fortunes of many peoples of the world.

Ilya Ehrenburg most likely had this in mind when he wrote about Armenia as being one of the countries, which for every thinking man are not only a source of deep esthetic pleasure, but of serious contemplation on the age-old roots and fate of art; that it is one of the countries at the sight of which one wants not only to bow one's head but to take one's shoes off and enter barefooted as one does a sanctuary in the East.

Over half of the books, which have survived, are kept at the Matenadaran, the Yerevan depository of ancient manuscripts, and the rest are scattered like our people all over the world.

Anyone entering the hall of manuscripts in the Matenadaran feels the silence of the thirty centuries of our people's history, a silence which is more eloquent than words.

If the manuscripts were suddenly to break the silence, the mysterious halls of the Matenadaran would be filled with the sounds of prayers, shepherds' and ploughmen's songs, tolling bells, refugee's wails, clashing swords, galloping horsemen, mother's shrieks and roaring invaders...

They all have grown silent and still and turned to stone in the old folios.

The entire history of our people is concentrated in these halls — starting from the Hyksos invasion of Egypt in 1600 B.C. down to the tragic events of 1915, A.D.

Every people and every individual has his own, unique and inimitable life-story.

And each of the manuscripts kept there has likewise a life-story of its own...

Only one thing joins them with unbreakable threads: each of them contains a tiny part of the history of the people who wrote them. Each of them has visible or invisible traces of the blood which the Armenians shed fighting for freedom and independence against tyranny and annihilation.

All kinds of manuscipts are kept here: the words of 5th century historians and philosophers, Armenian translations of the theoretical works by Aristotle, Platon and Xenon, astronomical and mathematical works by Ananya Shirakatsi, and the *Consolation in Fevers* by the medieval Armenian physician Mkhitar Heratsi, the *Book of Lementations* by Grigor Narekatsi (10th century) and the manuscripts of songs by Sayat-Nova...

They vary in size and appearance, from a 5th century ivory-bound Gospel, the weighty *Homilies of Mush,* down to a minute Calendar weighing 19 grams which can only be read through a magnifying glass.

There are luxurious editions of ecclesiastic canonical books, which are of little interest to science, and there are plain-looking collections of songs, chronicles, as well as collected works on philosophical and scientific matters which are of enormous value.

There is most likely no sphere of erudition which is not to be found in the manuscripts of the Matenadaran.

One finds examples of all religious creeds and heresies, philosophy, history, medicine, mathematics, grammar, poetry and prose, botany, zoology, astronomy, chemistry, anatomy, geography, geology, music, alchemistry, painting and aeronautics. There are numerous dictionaries and grammar books, geographical maps and calendars, drawings and books of arithmatic problems, text-books on preparing dyes, inks, and parchments...

Alongside books by Armenian physicians are translations of books by Galen, Nemesius, Nyssa and Avicenna; books by Narekatsi and Nerses Shnorhali; the oldest translations of the works of Homer, Cato, Ovid, Aesop, Olympiodorus and Menander; the Armenian account or version of the History of Alexander by Pseudo-Callisthenes (together or with Khachatur Kecharatsi's wonderful verses — "Kaphas") which are of world significance.

There are translations of the Italian medieval fables and stories, The Song of Roland, Paris and Vienna, works by Firdowsi, Nizami, Rustaveli, and Fizuki, and poems by Navoi, the Uzbek poet, all of which were recorded in 1494, in the poet's life-time.

The Armenian ancient manuscripts contain so many different subjects that it would be even difficult to arrange them into separate categories. Take for example, History of Translations of the Bible and History of the Balloon.

But what do these old Armenian manuscripts tell us?

So as not to disturb the mysterious silence of the hall again, let's only leaf through books which are being studied by the research workers at the Matenadaran today.

Indeed, what could the scribes from an Armenian monastery which was lost in the backwoods and constantly being plundered and destroyed, tell man of the 20th century who had seen and heard of everything? Man who knows Einstein and the Quantum Theory, who has landed on the Moon, who has transplanted hearts, and who had thoroughly digested the theory of Hegel and Marx?

It is well-known that the most fundamental question and the basis and essence of philosophy and science is the problem of the correlation of matter and ideas, and depending on the answer, one may determine the place occupied by the philosopher or scientist in the progress of human thought.

So, let us listen with admiration and awe to what Grigor Tatevatsi, the 13th century Armenian philosopher, writes on the cognition and reflection of the world and on the relation of ideas and matter: "We cognize (the world) little by little, acquiring knowledge to a greater or lesser extent, according to the changes taking place in matter.

Our knowledge follows the essence of matter because first *matter* exists and only then our *cognition*..."

Or: "if everything you saw were true, it would mean that it is not the mind that follows matter, but the contrary, which is quite wrong, since the constant does not follow the inconstant, but is only reflected in it. After all, footprints come after feet and not before, a shadow follows a body and not the contrary. It is hence clear that it is not thought that verifies the essence of matter but the

14—Seven songs about Armenia

reverse". The world is cognizable, writes Tatevatsi, because "by thinking wisely we penetrate into all the spheres of the world and nothing can hide from the light of wisdom".

One had to be bold and daring to think and write in such a way in the Middle Ages! No punishment, king or even God Himself could ever frighten or overpower such a thinker.

"The mind is a bold and fearless judge! It does not fear God because it is free; it does not feel shame because it keeps itself hidden; it doesn't take bribes because it does not need them; it is not ignorant because it always scrutinizes everything. That is why it judges truly and correctly..."

Tatevatsi was fortunate that our Church neither went in for vicious persecutions and inquisitions like the Catholic one, nor saw the like of San Benito and the terrible fires! Otherwise he would have been burnt as a heretic long ago for his "daring and insane" ideas.

Here we may read what the Armenian philosophers and scientists wrote about the globe and Sun and the eclipses of the Sun and Moon back in the fifth and seventh centuries — heretics expressing such ideas were burnt on the bonfire ten centuries later, in the 15-16th centuries...

This is what we read in *Interpretations of the Genesis* by Yeghisheh, the 5th century Armenian philosopher and scientist: "When the Moon is in the upper hemisphere, and the Sun in the lower, that is, when they are both on the same axis, the Sun cannot illumine the Moon simultaneously and an eclipse of the Moon takes place".

And here is what Ananya Shirakatsi, the great 7th century philosopher, astronomer and mathematician, wrote: "The earth reminds me of an egg. Just as the round yolk is in the middle of the egg, surrounded by egg-white and covered by the shell, so the round Earth is surrounded by air and enveloped on all sides by the sky". Elsewhere he wrote that every living being is subject to decay, and the seeds of a living creature emerge from decay; the world continues to exist as a result of this contradiction.

In the *Book of the Law* by Mkhitar Gosh, the 12th century scholar and fabulist, we read: "God created human nature to be free; but man is forced by his need for soil and water to serve masters. And I consider that he is fully justified to be free of his masters and live wherever he likes..."

Grigor Tatevatsi affirms and expands this idea: "Common people deserve leniency and charity, for they do not commit a crime willfully but because of their poverty. He steals, as the parable tells us, to appease his hungry belly, whereas a prince commits a crime of his own free will for he is in need of nothing, and that's why he should be doubly punished".

Tatevatsi was an extraordinarily profound thinker with a most varied range of interests. He first advanced the credos of the greatest thinkers of the future in many philosophical questions. Here is what he says about the origin of man, the role of labour in converting a four-legged creature into a two-legged one: "Man's head is raised, so that his tongue and hands can serve his thoughts and labour. For if his head was lowered, and his hands were pressed against the ground, he wouldn,t be able to work, and he would have to have a long tongue and thick lips to pick up food. In such a case his tongue wouldn't serve his thoughts as it does now..."

The philosopher and scientist, Mateos Djughaetsi went on developing this idea in the 15th century. "Animals do not need hands because they do not have any creative ability. But man has intelligence and wisdom which require the use of his hands. That is why he stood on his hind legs, and raising his two front ones, converted them into instruments of labour..."

In the Middle Ages when man was considered sinful and base, the views expounded by Tatevatsi on man's perfection sounded like a hymn to man.

Speaking of the three stages of the soul's development, which are vegetal, sensory and intellectual, and of the transition from the imperfect stages to a perfect intellectual one, Tatevatsi asserts that the latter can only be found in a perfect being such as man.

One could quote endlessly from the works of other historians and philosophers, such as David Anhaght (the Invincible), Yeznik Goghpatsi, Grigor Magistros, Hovhan Vorotnetsi and Simeon Djughaetsi...

However, even the few quoted here are sufficient to show that the wellknown and unknown Armenian scholars, who referred to themselves as "unworthy" and "ignorant" and lived in the most remote corners of poor old Armenia, were leading scientists and philosophers of their time and expressed thoughts, which many centuries later were considered "daring innovations" even in civilized countries.

It is not surprising that foreign invaders first attacked the centres of our culture and destroyed book depositories, killed learned monks and scribes, and devastated and burned manuscripts, hoping to dim the light radiating from them.

But our people, who dearly love books, gave their lives to save not only our Armenian manuscripts but also many Slavonic, Persian, Greek, Jewish, Indian, Latin, Arabic, Georgian and other ones, which are now kept at the Matenadaran in Yerevan and are the envy of many book depositories in the world...

Many works by Ancient Greek, Assyrian and other scientists and philosophers, which were lost over the centuries, are now becoming available again to the world, thanks to the Armenian translations which have remained intact.

They include such works as *The Chronicle* by Eusebius of Caesarea, the famous 4th century Greek historian, the book *On Nature* by the Greek philosopher Zeno the Stoic, the works of Theon of Alexandria and Philo Judaeus, fragments from *Botany* by Dioscorides, the mathematical work *"Ketable Nejab"* by Avicenna, many sections of the *History of Alexander the Great* by Pseudo Callisthenes, and others...

Almost all the Armenian historians have written about the numerous cultural centres, libraries, schools and universities of ancient and medieval Armenia and mostly about their being destroyed by invaders.

Here is what one scribe wrote: "Tamerlane gave an order to seize and destroy a vast number of ancient manuscripts, some of which he carried away to Samerkand".

"In 1178, a library with ten thousand manuscripts was burnt to the ground in the city of Baghaberd by invading Seljuks",— another scribe informs us. This is how in 1386 the scribe Akop describes the ordeal endured both by him and his teacher, philosopher Hovhan Vorotnetsi, during the Mongolian invasion: "This mansucript was finished in a bitter and sorrowful year..."

After invading Armenia, the Mongols captured the Vorotan Fortress, and Vorotnetsi, pursued by the enemies, was forced to escape. The scribe Akop continues: "And I followed him, heavily burdened by a bag containing papers and a copy of the manuscript, ink and a pen, reading and writing as much as I could amidst many difficulties and hardships, for whenever I began writing I couldn't finish".

On the last page of the manuscript, No 823, writen in 1266, there is a drawing which is interesting in that it has no connection whatsoever to the subject of the manuscript.

An old man wearing a purple mantle is lying on the floor and blood is flowing out of his chest. Blood-stained swords and spears are strewn by his side. Under the picture is the young scribe's memorial inscription in which

he asks the reader of the manuscript, "to remember and pray for my spiritual father and teacher slain by foreign invaders before my very eyes".

The letters are stained with tears and his handwriting is jerky. Evidently, the scribe noticed this and apologized to the reader: "In the last pages of the book there are many errors, and the letters are large and uneven. Since my sorrow is profound and I am the most unworthy of my master's pupils".

Each conqueror tried to annihilate not only the people, but, first and foremost, their spriritual culture.

The people fled their homeland, taking with them books, which had been saved from destruction.

And along with the cultural centres in Armenia, new centres were founded in Theodosia, Amsterdam, Venice, Jerusalem, Lvov, and many other places including the distant Philippines.

Armenian manuscripts have been written or sent to almost every country of the world.

Every time our enemies tried, like a storm, to uproot the tree of Armenian culture, its seeds were scattered all over the world and gave rise to new shoots.

The centres of Armenian culture outside Armenia gave a new lease of life to the libraries and universities in Armenia. Manuscripts were bought and brought back to Armenia; new ones were written and new libraries and universities were built.

"In the year 1235, my wife Khorishan and I built this library and chapel in memory of our daughter Mamakhatun", reads Prince Vachutyants' inscription on the wall of the Monastery of Saghmosavank.

There are not only many cultural centres in Armenia but also many literary schools, each of which has its own features...

The best known among them are the Shirak School (Ani, Haghpat, Sanahin), the Syunik School (Noravank, Gndevan, Gladzor, Tatev), the Cilician (Hromkla, Sis, Drazark, Akner), the Crimean (Kapha, Surkhat, Kerch), the Van School (Narek, Van, Akhtamar, Khizan), the Karin, Yerzinka, Djugha and the Polish school.

The Etchmiadzin book depository is undoubtedly one of the oldest centres of Armenian letters. Founded in the 5th century, it has collected the manuscripts of the Saghmosavank Cloister and other monasteries since the 15th century and is rightly considered our most important despository of manuscripts.

How many people worked on each of the twenty five thousand manuscripts which have remained intact to this day! How many people wrote or transcribed them, stored and saved them from destruction for readers of the future!

Take, for instance, the scribes, humble, poor people, to whose legendary hard work and devotion we owe these depositories.

We may learn interesting facts about their lives, fates, thoughts and feelings from the scanty memorandums.

As a rule, the scribes avoided writing about themselves, and if they did, it was with the utmost modesty: they referred to themselves as "most unworthy" and 'the first among the ignorant and the last among the wise". Their life was hard and their work exhausting but they did not write about this. Instead, they wrote about the great consolation and reward for all their difficulties — the book.

They rarely wrote about the hard work involved in preparing the parchment, acquiring dyes and inks or the years and decades they toiled over the manuscript.

They did not write about how many of them went blind and died prematurely.

They were the poorest in the monasteries, existing on bread and water and suffering from the cold, dampness and diseases.

They had to suffer greatly to save the manuscripts from the plunderers and fires. Many were killed in their cells as they worked. Many led terrible lives, wandering through towns and villages, countries and states to buy back the manuscripts which had been captured by invaders.

How hard it was for them to make several copies of boring canonical books and theological treatises! How many times they were deceived and left unpaid on completing the manuscript and dismissed from a monastery, penniless!

How many scribes lost their lives in exile or were killed by enemies while trying to save the manuscripts!

The manuscripts from the Sanahin and Haghpat monasteries were hidden in the gorges and caves of Lori during the Mongolian invasions.

The enemies surrounded them and began torturing the monks to make them reveal the hiding place. But three fanatic senior clergymen and twelve junior ones proudly retorted with a line from the Gospel: "Do not give holy things to dogs, and throw not pearls to pigs!"

The memorial statue to these clergymen, known as "The Three Crosses" is supposedly still intact somewhere near the Haghpat-Sanahin monasteries.

This incident was not coincidental or unique. Many fanatic scribes and learned monks risked their lives to save the manuscripts which they regarded as holy things and dearly-loved living creatures.

Sometimes childless Armenian families "adopted" a manuscript, as they would a child, and in their wills asked the authorities of a monastery or library to take charge of their "adopted child".

Indeed, the manuscript was a beloved living creature for the Armenians and an indomitable foe for their enemies Otherwise why did a certain Persian Shah seize a manuscript and put it in chains?

The scribes wrote about the manuscript as though it were a living being and considered it that the best reward for all their sufferings was to be able to sign their name in a corner of the last page of the manuscript.

The boldest scribes left memorandums in which they expressed their thoughts and feelings and sometimes wrote verses or drew themselves at the feet of a famous scholar or poet. These short memorandums are wise and full of popular wit.

Mesrop Mashtots, the inventor
of Armenian letters (IVe».

In one manuscript there is a description of the Armenians' sufferings at the hands of the Mongols and of how some of them preferred war and death to shameful slavery.

The scribe added his own comment in the margin: "it is better to die with a clear conscience than live with lowered eyes".

Another scribe, who was concerned about how the poor peasants drowned their sorrows in drink after handing over their harvest to princes and monasteries, gave them a list of twelve "harmful effects of drunkeness". But then, apparently sensing that this would not help and that this would still go on drinking wine, he resorted to more practical advice — how to drink without getting drunk: "Chew seven almonds on an hungry stomach and then after every glass chew two quince seeds". This is even worth trying today!

Describing how an Armenian peasant murdered a Seljuk Khan, notorious for his atrocities, the scribe adds his own idea: "He who kills a rabid dog is innocent".

In one of the numerous Armenian translations of Aristotle (over three hundred in all), one suddenly reads in the margin alongside the deep philosophical thoughts: "On fleas: pour the blood of a goat into a large shallow bowl and place it by one's side. In this way you will rid youself of fleas". Nowadays it seems strange to connect Aristotle with fleas but in those days it was quite natural and understandable. The scribe was constantly plagued by fleas as he worked in his stuffy cell with its earthen floor. He could not work and it was of paramount importance that he got rid of the fleas in order to finish Aristotle's book.

Facts of this kind vividly depict the contradictions prevailing in old Armenia.

In another manuscript, the scribe made a mistake, crossed it out, corrected it and added the following remark: "If one starts talking to a scribe, such errors are inevitable". Obviously, someone talkative interrupted him at work, and perhaps shared his troubles which seemed more important than the contents of the manuscript.

Of great interest are the scribes' commentaries on the subjects copied by them. One of them, copying a book by David Anhaght, a 5th century Armenian neo-Platonic philosopher, was dissatisfied with the philosopher's very complex turn of phrase: "O, philosopher David",— he remarks in the margin of the manuscript,— "couldn't you write a little more simply, so that we, too, could understand something!"

Another scribe, copying the translation of the *Grammar* by Dionysius Thrax, was angered by the pedantic and obsolete formal declensions and conjugations of the verb "to forge" which took up dozens of pages of the manuscript, halted for a moment and commented: "O, brother reader, I am tired of forging; forge yourself if you want to",— and went on to another section of the manuscript.

Tens of thousands of scribes in Armenia worked on manuscripts and their memorandums make up whole volumes.

Thanks to their diligent work we now possess the greatest of treasures of the Armenian people — the riches of the Matenadaran. And I very much hope to see a statue of a scribe in front of the gate of Matenadaran alongside the statues of our philosophers, historians, scientists and writers...

> My hand will droop, wither and die,
> Only my scripts will stay alive...

This was the scribes' sole consolation for devoting their whole life to this back-breaking labour and toil...

And though their hands have turned to ash, their scripts have survived and are now kept in the new Matenadaran in Yerevan...

Neglecting themselves, their health and life, the scribes were interested only in the fate of their manuscripts. In most of the memorandums, they beseech their readers of the present and future to look after their "offspring". Here is an example of such a memorandum:

> "Ay, my readers, listen to me,
> I've an advice to bequeath ye.
> I leave my book as a behest,
> To cherish it and read it best.
> Redeem it back whenever thralled,
> Keep it with care and clear of mould.
> Let no water or candle wax
> Drip on and harm a single page.
> Do not leaf it with moist fingers,
> Or tear pages as it withers...

The scribes were not afraid of death but of dying without finishing the manuscript.

The eighty-six-year-old scribe, Hovhannes Mangasarents, was so afraid of this that he somehow held his trembling right hand with his left so as to complete the last manuscript in crooked letters. He died with only the memorandum unwritten... This was finished by the young scribe Zakaria who wrote the following about his teacher: "For seventy-two years, winter and summer, day and night, he copied manuscripts. He completed one hundred and thirty two. And in his old age, when his sight had deteriorated and his hands trembled, he with great difficulty completed St. John's Cospel and afterwards could no longer hold a pen".

The Matenadaran contains many manuscripts which were "mutilated in battle" — true soldiers who were victims of the Armenian Genocide and were miraculously saved from death. The binding and parchments of some of them were torn, others were half burned in fires or conflagration, some were drowned in rivers, others were cut to pieces with knives, some were chained, attempts were made to scrape off the Armenian letters on others and inscribe new ones...

Among the "mutilated" manuscripts of the Matenadaran, there are also many "heroes" and victims of the 1915 Genocide...

Many of the damaged manuscripts are now being restored, but others were so petrified by the horror that they turned into stone and will never be able to reveal their secrets.

Sometimes in the remote past manuscripts, which had been half-burnt, damaged by swords and soaked in water beyond repair, were buried like soldiers killed in action, but nobody dared to bury these sacred relics in the ground so they were put in vaults like dear relatives.

Among such long-suffering manuscripts was the "Homilies of Mush" which had a history similar to that of our people.

This manuscript was copied in the Armenian town of Mush (now in Turkey) by the scribe, Vardan Karnetsi. He took three years to copy it and completed it in 1204. This vast manuscript weighs 32 kg (without its binding). About 600 calves were slaughtered for its 607 large parchment pages.

The "memorandums" of this giant manuscript cover a great variety of subjects, which are mostly tragic: the battle of Basen in 1204, at which the allied forces of Armenia and Georgia utterly defeated the invading Seljuk hordes of Rukn-ed-Din; the murder of the owner of the manuscript (for whom it was written); the story as to how it was taken captive and how the Armenians made "door-to-door" collections among the villages and monasteries to raise the necessary ransom of 4000 pieces (about 20 kg of silver) to retrieve the manuscript and bring it back to the monastery of Mush.

Here in this monastery the manuscript was kept in re-

lative safety for about seven hundred years, that is, save a couple of fires and dozens of miner invasions during which the manuscript was hidden in the cellars of the monastery.

During World War I it was again threatened with total destruction. The Russian troops pulled back from the Caucasian front and the Turkish hordes advanced unhindered, destroying everything living and valuable on their way.

But the manuscript was saved by two starving Armenian women refugees from the smoldering plundered monastery. They took turns in carrying this heavy burden (weighing over 32 kgs) on their backs. After exhausting themselves, they divided it in half and wrapped one half in cloths and buried it in the churchyard of the Armenian church of Erzerum, and carried the second half safely to Etchmiadzin.

Time passed and the second half of the manuscript was found and given to the Matenadaran by a Polish officer in the Russian army.

At last the two halves of this long-suffering manuscript, whose history is similar to our people's, were joined in their native land and now live in peace. However, like our people, this manuscript is not complete: seventeen of its parchment pages are in Italy, where they were once brought (probably in the Middle Ages), and are now kept in one of the libraries of Venice...

The menfolk were also courageous in those hard times. When fleeing from the Turks, they carried away the giant gate of the monastery of Mush — a masterpiece of Armenian wood carving of the 12th century — to Eastern Armenia. They literally put it on their shoulders and took it to Yerevan, where it is now exhibited in the History Museum. This gate later served as a model for modern Armenian craftsmen making the door of one of the exhibition halls of the Matenadaran where the *Selected Speeches* is now kept just as it was in the Monastery of Mush in the past.

... Our people has lost innumerable cultural treasures during its centuries-old history.

Christianity destroyed the pagan literature and art, the heretics fought against all that was Christian in nature, and the foreign invaders destroyed both.

However, in spite of this, we still have an inexhaustible amount of valuable literature, including the pagan legends preserved in the book of the *History of Armenia* by Movses Khorenatsi, the father of our historiography, and his famous *Lament;* Yeghisheh's fiery "About Vardan and the Armenian War"; wise medieval parables; the splendid hymns by Narekatsi and Shnorhali; lyrical odes by medieval bards and our unmatched "hayrens"; numerous verses by known and unknown minstrels and those by Naghash Hovnatan and Sayat-Nova. It is with a feeling of pride that one leafs through the centuries-old book of our poetry, immortal creations by immortal creators, starting from the books of our first historians and poets down to the dazzlingly vivid medieval poetry and new 20th century literature.

But at the same time one feels sad when one remembers that if these books written by Armenian writers over the centuries are still topical, it means that nothing has changed, in Armenia; the same misfortunes and suffering, the same unsolvable and complex problems and pointless task of getting rid of them, in short, everything that caused these books to be written, is still with us.

Just open and leaf through one of the books of our age-old literature such as the *Lament* by Khorenatsi or one by Issahakian, Varouzhan or Terian...

They are all unique, but in essence they are the same: they mainly describe the grief and sufferings of our people, the struggle against foreign invaders and tyrants, and faith in a bright future. It is as though all those works from the 5th century onwards were written by one and the same author — a sensitive and wise eye-witness of all the people's centuries-old sufferings and misfortunes.

Here is what Khorenatsi writes in his *Lament: I mourn* for thee, homeland of Armenians, for you are deprived of your kings and clergy, your councillors and teachers; troubled is your peace, destroyed is your faith and your superstition is steeped in ignorance. Faced with struggles from within, and dangers from the outside, no counselor can give you good advice. Your governors keep no law and order and are cruel-hearted; your beloved are betrayed, your enemies strengthened and your faith is being traded for an easy life..."

The same idea is expressed by Yeghisheh, Yeznik and all the other historians. It is to be found in the 6th and

7th centuries during the Arab invasions. It is expressed by Aristages Lastivertsi, the 11th century historian...

Khorenatsi closes his history with his *Lament,* whereas Lastivertsi opens his book with one...

> We are facing days of hardships,
> And misfortunes rushing in heaps...
> People deviate from what is right,
> Plunging into an aweful plight...
>
> There's no justice, law and order,
> And corruption is widely spread..
> That's why every wild invader
> Drives us away from our land...
>
> Dangers of war give us no-rest,
> Both from within and without...
> Havoc and death from East and West,
> Woe and distress from North and South...

There is a fine medieval poem,— probably written by Grigor Akhtamartsi, a 16th century poet,— which touches the problem of the eternal link and contradiction between life and death, of man being a mortal being and having to pass away without seeing his wishes fulfilled or enjoying his life in this world...

Undoubtedly, one may find a similar poem in every literature. However, each poem adds the local colour and images, characteristic of his country and people to this eternal theme.

One compares life and death to the sea and a ship;

another, to the desert sands and camel caravans, and so on.

Akhtamartsi (or our people) gave this eternal theme a new meaning, making it doubly significant by linking it to a theme, ever topical for our people, of forced exile, of being made to abandon one's sacred home and vineyard planted with one's hands forever. Just as the enemy and the foreign conqueror compels one to abandon one's own home and vineyard and seek refuge in foreign and unknown countries, so man is forced by approaching death to forsake life on earth...

> I carried stones by hand and coach,
> I walled and fenced my new vineyard,
> Yet with my eyes still on the watch,
> I'm told it's time to quit the world...
>
> Dug for water and out it burst,
> I built a spring in my vineyard,
> Yet quenching not my burning thirst,
> I'm told it's time to quit the world...
>
> I filled my jugs with the new wine,
> Squeezed from the grapes of my vineyard,
> Yet tasting not that wine of mine,
> I'm told it's time to quit the world...
>
> I built my home in my vineyard,
> Put into it my soul and heart,
> Then comes a voice bringing me word,
> To warn it's time to quit and part...

> How should I so quickly quit
> My own house and part with it?
> To have my spring for ever dried,
> And vines drooping and growing wild...?
>
> My mind grew weak, my thought withered,
> My heart broke up under its grief...
> I was borne out of my vineyard...
> Alas! that life should be so brief...!

New centuries arrived and so did new poets but the disastrous conditions of the country and people and themes chosen by poets remained the same. And this may be testified by the famous "Antouniner" and "Hayrenner" or lamentations and mournful songs of the exiled people which became the most popular folk-songs in the 16—18th centuries.

Here is one age-old lamentation, which was later reworked by Komitas, being still sung by Armenians today:

> I'm as downcast as that crumbling hut...
> With its shafts and logs just falling apart...
> Coming there to nest are the fowls wild...
> Let me go, be drowned with my horse and cart,
> And let the small fish pierce me part by part...
> Oh, you woeful guy...

And here is another "antuni", a mournful song, the like of which can hardly be found in world literature...

> I was a shoot of a peach tree,
> Rooted in rocks, firmly and free...
> Then people took and planted me
> In an alien, remote country...

They made liquids sweet and gummy,
To feed me up and nourish me...
Oh, take me there, where I should be,
Use thawing snow to water me...!

The fanatical love, which binds our people to its native language and spiritual culture, is truly amazing. They sensed instinctively that language and literature were their most powerful weapon in the eternal struggle for exitence.

Indeed, ever since the Armenian Alphabet was created, year after year, century after century, all the invading tyrants did everything they could to make the Armenians forget their mother tongue and to integrate and assimilate them. However, our small, helpless and lonely people waged a cruel struggle against them with the small regiment of the thirty-six letters of their alphabet. And they finally won the age-long, unequal battle and are now proudly writing the commandments of their new history with the same letters.

This was what we call "love for one's own mother tongue". It now seems an inexplicable metaphysical phenomenon, a feeling or an instinct which has the power to work miracles!

An interesting example of this profound feeling and striking phenomenon has been described by Remarque. One of his heroines, a Rumanian who had spent all her life in France, spoke French and had completely forgotten her native tongue, as she was in the agony of death, suddenly began speaking in her native tongue, which was unknown to everyone around her. Something similar happened in real life with one of the legendary heroes of the Civil War, an Armenian by the name of Haik Bzhishkian or "Gai" (in Russian) who was brought up and educated in Russia and had almost forgotten his native tongue... At a crowded meeting to celebrate the liberation of the Russian town of Simbirsk (the birthplace of Lenin) by the division under his command, in his excitement he suddenly began expressing his feelings in Armenian!

Otherwise, the tortured Armenian mothers could hardly have found the strength as they died in the death camps of Ter-Zor to trace the Armenian alphabet in the sand so that their children remained Armenian for the rest of their life.

I myself witnessed a similar incident. When I was in Moscow in 1957 or 1958 I received a telephone call from the Writers' Union informing me that two Mexican writers wished to talk to me. They were a married couple. The husband was a genuine Mexican Indian who only needed the Indian feathered head-gear and clay pipe to look like the chief of an Indian tribe. And his wife turned out to be an Armenian who had fled her home town in her early teens and through unforeseen cricumstances had ended up alone in the very heart of Mexico among the Indians. There, she later married an Indian and had her children. As time went by, she forgot her homeland and native tongue, and turned into an Indian. Her husband is now a literary critic and a University professor in Mexico. She is herself a well-known art critic and author of many books on Mexican and Latin American painting, sculpture and folk-dances. In a quiet room of the Writers' Union in Moscow, her husband showed me his wife's books, one after the other, which had been published in English, French and Spansh and spoke about his wife with undisguised pride. She herself remained silent. When we had looked at all her books, she suddenly swept them away with her hand and jerkily, in very poor Armenian, said: "All that means very little. Please read this". And with a trembling hand she extended to me a notebook bound in black leather, containing a poem scribbled in Armenian and entitled "An Exile's Dream". I quietly glanced through the verse and was on the point of giving a sincere judgement, as I always did, when suddenly noticed her expression. Her tearful eyes were blazing with such emotion and anticipation, as if she believed totally that this small weak verse scribbled in poor Armenian was the best and most important work of her life, that I was struck dumb and could say nothing.

Knowing the biography of this woman I could not help but admire this supernatural force which, even in this woman, who had spent all her life in Mexico, had helped her to keep her native language alive. What's more, it had been kept alive to such an extent that even the few unsuccessful lines scribbled in Armenian seemed to her much more sacred then all the serious books she had written in another language.

But enough of Mexico, let us return to Armenia.

One may often come across literate, semi-literate or

even illiterate Armenian craftsmen and peasants over the age of 60, who without letting their wives and families know, spend nights on writing the history of Armenia in verse in school copy-books (some 3000-5000 lines from the beginning to end), firmly convinced that they are doing the most important work of their life.

I have read dozens of Armenian "Odysseys" by semi-literate Armenian "Homers" without daring to express my real opinion of them. I was held back by my respect for their fanatical love and devotion to their native tongue and their sincere interest in the fate of our people.

There are probably few countries where one could find even semi-literate peasants reading books on the history of their people with as much interest as on works of art, or spending hours arguing passionately about various historical events.

Through centuries of history our people has created priceless treasuries of spiritual life, and especially of literature. And one main theme runs through our literature like a red thread — a thread which was woven into a red banner: that of our people's struggle for national liberation, and their unswerving hope and faith in a peaceful life and honest labour.

One might even say that we have never had literature for its own sake. From the very start it has been a powerful weapon of self-defense in the hands of our people in their struggle for a happy future.

Not only our language and literature were powerful weapons of self-defense and self-preservation but also the very fact that our alphabet was created, for apart from its literary significance, it pursued a political, diplomatic and even defensive course.

Small Armenia was forced for a long time to isolate and contain itself in order to safeguard itself and to avoid being swallowed by powerful neighbouring states and foreign invaders. In doing so, it emphasised its own identity.

When it was threatened by idolatrous Persia, it defended itself with the armour of Christianity guarding itself from the fire with the cross!

When Byzantium threatened to swallow Armenia under the pretext of making all Christian countries equal, Armenia at once produced its own interpretation of the Christian faith.

When Armenia realised that the Christian sermons (even its own Armenian Christianity) given in its churches in foreign languages could endanger the native tongue and existence of the people, it at once created its own Alphabet and written language so as to propagate its own Christianity in its own language and to safeguard its independence.

It was Mesrop Mashtots, the son of a peasant named Vardan from the village Hatsik, one of the greatest Armenian scholars and public figures of the 4th-5th centuries, who carried out the important mission of founding the Armenian Alphabet. After turning down a brilliant career at court and in the army, with the assistance of the Armenian King Vramshapuh and the Catholicos of all Ar-

ՀԱՄԱՆԵՐԵՆ ՆԱԿ
ՈՐ ՈՅԻ ՈՅԿ ԵՇ
ՅՈՂ Ռ ՄՐ ՆՈ Տ
ԸՆԱՆԵՆՅԻՐՈՑ Ի
ՓԱԿԲԵՅԱՆ ԴՈՏ
ՏԵՆ ԹԳ ԱՁ ՆԱ
ՓԱԲԱԱ ՀՈՆԵ ԵՀ
ԲԱԵԲԱ ՀԱՄ ՄԱՏ
ԱՐԹԻՆ : Դ : ՈՒ ԹԱ
ԹՈՒԵՏ ԵՌՈ : ԿԱ Ն
ՈՎ ՀԱԿ ԱՆ ՆԵ ՌՈՑ

Inscriptions on stones...

menians, Sahak Partev, one of the most highly educated people of his age, Mesrop Mashtots devoted his life to the difficult cause of creating the Armenian alphabet. In doing so, he helped the Armenian people more than Tigran the Great had done with the sword or Grigor Lusavoritch (the Illuminator) had done with the cross.

After receiving a general education in Armenia and after travelling across many countries and studying all the old and new languages of his time, he created an alphabet, which, incredible though it may seem, has not changed in the course of sixteen centuries and thanks to which I, an unworthy descendant of Mesrop Mashtots, am writing these lines.

The entire Armenian people came out to meet Mesrop Mashtots when he returned to Vagharshapat (the Armenian capital) with the new alphabet, the thirty-six courageous soldiers of the "book regiment" which has defended our identity for 1600 years. None of these letters perished in the numerous harsh and bloody battles but, instead, their ranks were supplemented by three other valiant soldiers, or, the letters "Yev", "O", "Fe" which "came over to our side" and joined our alphabet at a later date.

The first sentence written with the letters of our new alphabet is most characteristic of our people: "To know wisdom and instruction; to discern the words of understanding..."

This in itself expresses our people's unquenchable thirst for knowledge, not only of its own culture but also of all the best features in the cultures of other peoples, and their desire to share their cultural treasures.

Mesrop Mashtots is the greatest and most renowned public figure of our history and that is why his modest tomb in the village of Oshakan is a revered shrine in Armenia which has been visited by pilgrims from all over the world for sixteen centuries!

Incidentally, it was Mesrop Mashtots who first translated the Bible into Armenian (his translation is considered the best) and wrote the first "sharakan" (religious hymns), the first text-books and scientific essays. He opened the first Armenian schools, and became our first teacher and educator.

In as far as Christian historiography is concerned, Mesrop Mashtots' translation of the Bible is the most significant of his works. A Translators' Day was organised immediately after its completion which has been celebrated ever since in Armenia every autumn.

By the way, it was never a holiday simply for the Church or the upper class, but for the whole people — peasants and princes, craftsmen and soldiers, clergymen and scientists, readers and writers...

I remember the story Stepan Zorian told me about this occasion.

One day in late autumn a semi-literate glass-cutter came to the famous writer to glaze the window-panes of his house but did not complete his job during the day and said he would come the day after next.

"Perhaps you could come to-morrow or else we'll have to freeze for an extra day", said the writer.

"As much as I respect you, I cannot come tomorrow... It's Translators' Day. I'm going to Mashtots's grave to pay my respects".

"I at once felt ashamed that I had forgotten this",— reminisced the writer, "but at the same time I felt immensely proud of my people..."

... Mesrop Mashtots created the Armenian alphabet in 396 A.D., and only 55 years later, in 451, the Armenian letters waged their first battle for freedom against foreign invaders...

While the gunsmiths forged swords and spears, the historians and scholars wrote manuscripts on parchment. The latter was evidently dreaded more by the enemy. Otherwise, it's impossible to explain the hatred with which aggressor and conqueror destroyed the hearths of our culture, murdering the scribes and wrecking the manuscripts.

"It's better to be blind in the eyes than blind in the mind"; "Death not acknowledged is death, death acknowledged is immortality". These were two of the proverbs which in the 5th century inspired our writers and historians fighting for freedom.

One need harldy say that these words were more effective than the bows and arrows and swords and spears with which the Armenian soldiers were then armed.

... It was namely the spirit of the national liberation struggle and the desire for a peaceful life. which, in the 9th century, during the terrible Arab invasions, gave birth to the wise and vitally joyful epic poems, the *Dare-devils of Sassoun.*

Like the heroes of many epic poems, David of Sassoun (or David Sassountsi in Armenian) was armed with a magic weapon — a lightning sword, and like other heroes, he could easily defeat whole enemy armies with it if he wanted to.

But David of Sassoun seldom used his sword, and did so only when forced to, or when the people's "cup of patinece overflowed".

Even when Msra Melik and his formidable army invaded Armenia, David did not destroy his troops (like the heroes of many epics would have easily done).

And when, after all, he had killed the war-monger, Msra Melik, he freed all the Arab soldiers-peasants who had been forcibly dragged to the battlefield. As he bid farewell to them, he advised them to safeguard peace and never raise the sword against other peoples again:

> ... And what's the use of coming here
> With bows and arrows to alien lands?
> Haven't we, too, our homes so dear,
> Full of children and wrinkled hands...?
>
> Turn back and go the way you came,
> To Mesr, home, your own land...
> But if you tempt to do the same,
> And fall on us with arrows strained,—
>
> You'll have to face a rising hell,
> Sasna David, his lightning sword,

Ev'n if you dive deep down the well,
Or hide behind the mill-stone board...

And then only God knows indeed,
Who'll be sorry for all that goes...?
Not we, who'll strike, making no bid,
Since you made us to be your foes...

Whereas Grigor Narekatsi, the great 10th century poet and formidable volcano of human thoughts and emotions, in his prayers to God, placed man, made in God's image higher than God, three centuries later, the poet Frik, boldly entered into a dispute with God, condemning the world created by Him, where there are so many injustices, sorrows and evil things:

... Some are by birth noble and rich,
And some — beggars by heritage...
Some own hundreds of mules and steed,
Some have neither a lamb or kid...

Some own gold piles, a great many,
Some are deprived of a penny...
Some have hundreds of pearls to heed,
Others are stripped of a glass bead...

Some take and wear the purple robe,
Some find no shirt, nor do they hope,
Some may clear up a foul deed,
Some in justice never succeed...

Frik's poem, *Complaint,* reverberates with the same thunder with which Smbad Zarehavantsi, the leader of the medieval "Tondrak" heretics, flung the sacred chrism down the abyss of the Tatev mountains as a symbol of rebellion, honest labour and free love...

Frik was echoed by Mkrtich Naghash, one of the greatest poets of the 14th-15th centuries, who already divided the working people from their aggressive and plundering exploiters:

> ... And there were kings and noble lords,
> Who fought against their rival hordes,
> And blood they shed taking no heed,—
> Only out of human greed...

> ... Fathers and sons were drawn apart,
> Lovers forgot their love and heart,
> And fratricide spread like a creed,
> Only out of human greed...

Narekatsi and Frik were followed by a brilliant constellation of secular poets who illumined the gloomy sky of the Middle Ages; they eulogized the blooming tree of life instead of the crucifixion, and the fragrant odour of spring flowers instead of incense.

The lyrical poems about love and nature which now seem innocently amusing, were in those days considered too daringly and dangerously opposed to religious dogmatism, connonical poetry and the "personality cult" of God.

This lyrical poetry marked the beginning of the real Renaissance, the first signs of which were already apparent in Armenian literature, art and philosophy several centuries before the European Renaissance.

Valery Bryusov, the celebrated Russian poet, had this to say: "Armenian medieval poetry is one of the outstanding triumphs of the human spirit ever known to world history... It should be the duty of every educated person to get to know Armenian poetry, as it is for him to know the Greek tragedians, Dante and Shakespeare..."

The *Book of Lamentations* by Grigor Narekatsi marked the first signs of the Armenian Renaissance...

And one should not forget that Narekatsi lived 300 years before Dante!

And the only reason why he did not become as famous as Dante, and even today is little known to the civilized world, is that the Armenians did not have a statehood, which frequently compels other peoples to join the culture of a nation, or serves as a high pedestal above which the cultural treasures of any given people may be clearly seen by the world at large.

Narekatsi's *Book of Lamentations,* which deals in essence with man's inner world is the first of its kind in Armenian poetry, and probably in world poetry. It explores the deep recesses of the human soul, the duality of man, the relationship between the mortal and immortal, the perfect and imperfect, and, finally, the problem of the relationship between man and God...

Narekatsi lived at a time when, as he put it, *the present is non-existent, the past unknown, the future uncer-*

tain, and man was surrounded on all sides by traps and adversities, and seems to share Narekatsi's fears:

> If I see soldiers, I just think of death,
> If a messenger — of a frightening news,
> If a learned man — of a perilous bill,
> And if a lawyer — of slander and curse...!

From whom could one seek protection if one's kings were only skilled at the art of murder?

And considering that the sorrows of the world, the people and every individual man were his own personal sorrow ("I am everyone, and what is in everyone, is in me"), Narekatsi wanted to be the only secrifice, and to die for the sake of everyone else just to save the world and mankind.

"In return for my mournful laments and sighs, have pity on the souls of others",—he prays to God, or as Paruir Sevak would have put it, "makes demands by pleading"

> Let all evil things,
> And hellish networks be crushed and dispersed...
> Let the secret lures come open to light,
> Let the foul tricks of plotters be split,
> Let the morbid weeds be scorched to their roots...
> Down with the cavils of the slanderers...
> Down with the swords of the murderers...
> Let the slanderers' tongues be struck dumb for good,
> Let all the false banners waving on the staffs,
> Be torn off and smashed to tiniest pieces,
> Let the tyrant's shaft be stopped in mid-air,

> Let the ship of fraud be wrecked on its way,
> And the gnawing teeth of rodents be pulled
> Deep out of their roots...!

And in as far as people's morals have always been in a lamentable state (and not only in Armenia!), Narekatsi's *BOOK* became *immortal*. It is always up-to-date, just as if it had been written for contemporary society.

Enraged and infuriated by the injustices and disorders in the world created by God, Narekatsi at times speaks angrily to God and even goes as far as to give Him advice:

> I pray Thee, hear me now, so that afterwards,
> Already too late,
> My prayers won't sink into void oblivion...
> ... Thus, take it for granted,
> To register me guilty in conscience,
> Than hear me call lies whatever you speak...

This is how he scorns the Almighty, but at once, becomes frightened of his own boldness and asks God to have mercy on him:

> O Lord, pardon me,
> To have thus forgotten all your benefits;
> Pardon me again!
> To have been so sinned with body and soul!
> O Lord, pardon me, the fool that I am,
> Being penitent to have gulled Thee thus,
> Pardon me, in *deed!*
> Spare me, to have thus detested Thy words,
> Do pardon my sins!
> Spare me, on my way to my agony,
> Have mercy on me, wretched as I am...

However, even at moments of great repentance and self-humiliation, Narekatsi instinctly feels that he, too, is God and immortal and proudly exclaims:

> Let nations hail it in its glorious march,
> Peoples hear of it, be sermoned by it,
> Let the doors of thought bear the stamp of it,
> And be it printed
> Deeply on the face of the human spirit...
> And although some day, as a mortal flesh,
> I shall pass away,
> But this book of mine will carry me on
> With the marching times...

And the devotion and reverential attitude of our people towards the immortal poem is the best testimony of their fanatic love for their language and literature.

In spite of the restrictions imposed by time, this book, which was written a thousand years ago, may truly be considered one of the most *contemporary* or, if you like, "up-to-date" books of the 20th century.

All Narekatsi's poetry is a fiery petition to God to grant perfection to man and one may well understand the admiration and interest shown to Narekatsi in all the countries where his poetry is being translated...

When you read Narekatsi's *Book* you really feel that *God* was created by man and not man by God, although after each of his daring outbursts, Narekatsi beseeches God to have pity on him being afraid of his wrath...

The most characteristic feature of his creative skill is the high spiritual tension and turbulent mood he crea-tes by constantly juxtaposing verbs:

I pray Thee, doom me not to be in my pains, but unfit to bear,
To mourn and not weep, to think and not sigh,
To be clouded and shower no rain,
To walk and not reach,
To plead earnestly and be answered not,
To beg, but receive nothing in return,
To make sacrifice and not feel the smell,
To look at Thy face, without avail...!

Here is how he describes man's inner struggle, his dual nature and spiritual contradictions:

And in either hand he carries two cups.—
One is full with blood, the other with milk...
Two censers flashing as bright as lightnings.—
One smelling fragrant, the other—flesh burnt...
Two bowls, designed for tasteful spices.—
One reserved for sweets, the other—for grief...
And two chalices, held on finger tips.—
One containing wine, and the other bile...!

This *Book* which is in the form of prayers but is theomachist in character, has been literally sanctified, or rather idolized by our people who consider it has magic power to heal the human body and soul. People's faith in the healing power of the *Book* became so great that for centuries it was customary to place it by a sick person's bed and read the following to the person:

If someone is struck by a mortal pain,
And is doomed to suffer,
Let him wish and hope to regain his health,
By praying to you on this sacred book...

17—Seven songs about Armenia

Narekatsi and Frik were followed by a new generation of secular poets, whose colourful, rich verses marked the triumph of living over dead and bloodless religious art. They wrote again about man and nature and infused life-giving blood into the withered veins of poetry.

"Your paradise is stronger than the cross". This is what Hovhannes Tlkurantsi, a 15th century poet, wrote of love, and then continued:

> Whenever man falls in love,
> He grows brighter, than the fire...
> He finds prayers and all sermons
> To be too dull to admire...,
>
> ... Your lips are bright, as bright as light,
> With liquid fire no one has got...
> Whoever sins by tasting it,
> Keeps it secret even from God...!

And if one remembers that the medieval poets, as a rule, lived and worked in monasteries, one can imagine the amount of courage shown by the "eccentric Hovhanness", as Tlkurantsi called himself, when he sat on the bank of a river in Spring, dreaming:

> How tenderly his arms he would twine
> Round her neck and drink his wine...

And what's more, suggesting a new funeral "ceremony":

> ... And let my corpse be washed with wine,
> Priests be replaced by singing horns...
> And being wrapped with leaves of pine,
> Be it buried in flowery lawns...

He was fortunate that, from the very first day of its existence, as history had willed it, the Armenian Church was of semi-secular character and administered by a council made up of an equal number of clergymen and laymen. Had the Armenian Church been as intolerant as the Catholic Church and had an inquisition, Hovhanness would certainly have been burnt at the stake like so many scientists, poets and philosophers in the Middle Ages...

Using this as a "precedent", the author of "Hayrens" Nahapet Kuchak was bold enough to ignore the Holy Church and... But let us listen to how he addresses his beloved:

> Your breasts are like snow-white temples,
> Your nipples glow like bright candles...
> Let me become a sexton there,
> To make prayers and ring the bells...

After being awoken by the sweet breath of the Renaissance, the body longed to be set free from the spiritual shackles of the Middle Ages in order to live, work and love freely:

> Just ever since of my birth-day,
> No priest heard me confess and pray,
> If I happened to cross his way,
> I would turn face and go away...
>
> And when I chanced a beauty's face,
> I ran to her with wide embrace,
> Made her bosom a chapel's grace,
> And to her breasts did I confess...!

Verses of this sort could obviously not be written in monasteries and Naghash Havnatan wrote his verses in freedom, preparing the way for the arrival of the greatest of Armenian bards — Sayat-Nova:

> Take up the glasses, fill them with red wine,
> Bring up the roast lamb, the dishes divine,
> Serve flowered pilaff, as a concord sign,—
>> Let us drink in one,
>> This sweet, tender wine!
>
> Let's sit on this lawn with water and grass,
> And drink the red wine together in mass,
> Let each get a rose from each one of us,
>> Let us drink in one,
>> This sweet, tender wine...!

... In the 17th century Armenia was divided once and for all between Turkey and Persia but despite this centuries-old nightmare, the Armenians were strong enough to produce such brilliant poets as Nahapet Kuchak, Naghash Hovnatan and Sayat-Nova who took Armenian poetry out of monastery for good.

Sayat-Nova was a poet, composer and musician. He wrote verses, put them to music and sang them, accompanying himself on the *kemani* (an eastern type of violin). What's more, he did so in several languages, five of which he knew well: Armenian, Georgian, Azerbaijan, Persian and Arabic, and the immortal and universal language of song with which he was, is and will always be present at all Caucasian feasts and in the hearts of lovers.

He was the son of a poor carpenter by the name of

Arutyun. He outstripped all the famous troubadours of his time and was appointed court poet to the Georgian king, Herakle II.

What more could a Caucasian poet wish for? But Sayat-Nova, an extraordinarily talented man and subtle and wise poet, who expressed the people's innermost feelings and hopes, despised the dull, and hypocritical atmosphere at court and was often criticized and persecuted for his proud and free spirit and "outspoken" songs.

His greatest suffering was caused by his daring love to the King's sister, Princess Ann, to whom he dedicated his best songs.

You're like a fairy among the fairest...
You have subdued me, you give me no rest,
None would ever find in the East or West,
One to be so fair in measure, my dear...!

People are just stunned as they glance at you,
Come near, let your pride be not so undue...
I'd like to please you, to be clear as dew,
And make you cheer up in music, my dear...!

My cares are doubled, that is what I mean,
I weep my own lot, that is what I mean,
Want to talk to you, that is what I mean,
Yet I can't be quenched in all this, my dear...!

Let the Khan kill me,— Sayat-Nova said,
Only for your sake I'd be better dead,
So that, dear, at least you could come and spread
Some handfuls of soil on my grave, my dear...!

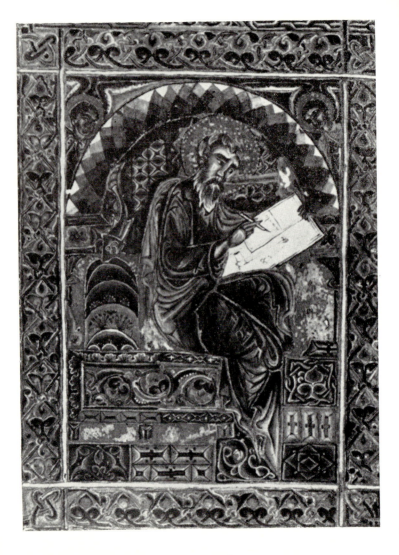

It is a pity that the dialect spoken by Armenians living in Tbilisi is gradually becoming unintelligible for contemporary readers and one is unable to get the full charm and depth of Sayat-Nova's verses.

It is essential to translate these unique poetic masterpieces into comtemporary Armenian, no matter how blasphemous and sacrilegious this might seem to our old dialect, the old-Armenian (Grabar) and Middle-Armenian languages.

> You're burning like fire!
> Spare me! No longer can I stand the heat...!

Had Sayat-Nova only written love songs, he would still be one of the best lyrical poets of the world.

However, he also graced us with unique verses about the happy and unhappy aspects of this transitory life of ours, such as *"Our World is like a Window",* which provides enough evidence to consider him one of the wisest poets of the world.

Our world is like a window,— I am all tired surveying it,
One seems to look and break his heart,— I am all tired deploring
it...
Today is worse than yesterday,— I am all tired expecting it,
People always differ in heart,— I am all tired displaying it...

The world belongs to none of us,— that's what always the wisemen
say,
I wish I were a thrush and fly,— all these gardens have tired
me up...

..Sayat-Nova had this to say,— I'm blocked, my cares are too many,
I am deprived of my sweet days,— the bitter ones are too many,
That's why I weep as a thrush does,— weeds in roses are too many,
They hinder them to bloom in time,— picking them up has tired me up...!

Cunning spongers at court soon succeeded in revealing the secret of he poet's lofty and unhappy love and he was forced to take holy orders and sent to the monastery of Haghpat.

> That's why all truth is now blocked...
> Lies are spreading,— they're too many...!

This was what Sayat-Nova flung sadly in the face of his time but despite his sufferings, he remained, however, magnanimous and unresentful:

> If one gives you the bitter bile,
> You, in return, serve him with sweets, Sayat-Nova...

In these lines the "people's servant" as he called himself in one of his songs expresses an important feature of the Armenian people who had not become embittered after so many sufferings but had remained kind-hearted and altruistic.

They have remained true to the old prayer of Armenian mothers, later put into verse by Avetik Issahakian:

> Let God first of all keep under his guard
> The sick and the poor and the traveller mild...
> Let Him reach you last and be on thy guard,
> Wherever you are, my only poor child...!

Every people has many proverbs and sayings about hospitality and sincerity but the Armenian proverb: "My house belongs not to me, but to the one who opens its door" — acquires a special meaning when you remember that it is said by Armenians whose houses have been robbed, destroyed and set on fire countless times by "uninvited guests" who came into their house.

Sayat-Nova appealed to the world with a famous song in which he expressed the sincere wish of our long-suffering people: "Love the scriptures, love the pen, love books".

And today these words are written in gold letters on the walls of our schools, libraries and bookshops. They, as it were, carry on the first sentence written with the letters of the Armenian alphabet: *To know wisdom and instruction; to discern the words of understanding"*.

This thought has run throughout the entire history of our people: whatever happens, love your language, literature and spiritual culture. How else can one explain why there are so many cultural centres, schools, libraries and medieval universities in Armenia and so many old manuscripts and books?

The early 19th century writer and teacher, Khachatur Abovian, is rightly considered the founder of the new Armenian literature and the new literary language, known as "Ashkharabar", which could be understood by the simple people. The son of a peasant from the village of Kanaker near Yerevan, from his early childhood Abovian witnessed the arbitrary rule of the Perisan Khans and

Pharashes who pillaged, plundered, killed, beat and abducted women.

Abovian later expressed all he saw with great feeling in his novel *The Wounds of Armenia,* in which he linked the hopes of liberating the Armenian people with Russia.

However, Abovian was not the first to raise this issue.

Russia was first mentioned in Armenian manuscripts in a history book by Movses Kaghantkatvatsi (9th century): "At that time an unknown people called *Ruziks* appeared from the north. More than three times they swept like a storm down to the Caspian sea and reached Partav, the capital of the Albans..."

Besides the numerous chronicles about Russia, Armenian historians such as Asoghik, Stepanos Orbelian and Kirakos Kantsaketsi subsequently wrote about Russia and the Russian people.

Ever since Russia and the Russian State came into being, the Armenians repeatedly took up arms and helped it fight its enemies (especially in the Kievian period), and they sometimes sought assistance from it. As early as in the 12th century Grigor Tutevordi, the father superior of Sanahin monastery, describing Armenia's desperate position, advised: "Send protests to the emperor, confer with the nation of the Franks, Assyrians and the glorious Russian church, revered for its Christianity, and ask them the assistence you need".

At the same time, in the 12th-13th centuries, one of the best works of medieval Russian literature, *The History of Boris and Gleb,* was translated into Armenian.

Subsequently, Armenian manuscripts were full of references to Russia and many translations of Russian books were made, especially in the 17th-19th centuries, when the Armenians linked their hopes of liberation from foreign tyranny with Russia.

The numerous translations of this period included "The Origin of the Russian State", "Concerning the House of the Rurikovich", "The Laws of Peter the Great", "The 1807 War between Nesvidayev and Mahmout Pasha", "The Most Important Decrees of the Russian Tsars (1795-1825)".

Peter the Great, reforming Russia, attracted progressive-minded, skilled and talented people. He could not help noticing the diligent Armenian people who were being persecuted by Persia and Turkey and he did everything to help as many Armenian carftsmen, builders and bibliophiles as possible to emigrate to Russia.

"Take care of the Armenians as much as you can and eleviate their hardships so that as many as possible may move to Russia",— he wrote in his Decree of March 2, 1711.

In another decree, addressing General Kropotov, Peter the Great writes: "Give the Armenians whatever help they need because we have taken this people under our special imperial protection".

Peter the Great gave the Armenians all kinds of previleges so it was not by mere chance that during and after his reign more than half a million Armenians moved to Russia, settling first in Petersburg and Moscow and then in towns founded by Armenian emigrants such as Novy Nakhichevan, Armavir and Grigorioupolis.

The persecuted Armenian people felt drawn towards, and believed in "Christian Russia" ever since the 12th century.

A striking example of this whole-hearted love and faith (which in spite of great disappointments did not waver even at the most tragic moments of our history), is to be found in a story by the Armenian writer Vahe Haik a witness of the 1915 Genocide entitled "Uncle Must Come".

Everyone knows that not all "uncles" are good people and that there's a world of difference between the Russian Decembrists liberating Armenia from the Persian yoke and "Uncle" Paskevich drowning Poland in a blood-bath; between Nalbandian and his teacher and friend Chernishevsky and the Russian gendarmes who convicted them. And during World War I, a most tragic time for the Armenian people, when the most progressive public figures of Russia-Lenin, Kirov, Gorky and Bryusov were offering us help, the reactionary tsarist general and later enemy of the revolution, Yudenich was secretly plotting to found a Euphratian Kazak state on the deserted land of dying Armenians...

This sincere age-old love and faith of the Armenian people for Russia has often taken the form of military and state alliances. Such was the case during and after the reign of David-Bek until Eastern Armenia was liberated from the Persian yoke.

Khachatur Abovian was among the first to give poli-

Ancient mosaics near the Temple of Garni...

tical meaning to that age-old love which our people have unwaveringly adhered to ever since. Shortly after the liberation of Yerevan from Persian domination, which Abovian had witnessed and participated in, he first heard about Pushkin's poetry from the exiled Decembrist officers, and for the first time saw a production of Griboyedov's "The Woe from Wit" in the old Yerevan fortress. Then he went to work as a secretary at Etchmiadzin, the holy seat of the Catholicos of all Armenians. In the monastery there he became acquainted with Fredrich Parrot, a professor at the University of Dorpat, with whom he shortly afterwards climbed to the top of Mt. Ararat.

It was hard to climb Ararat in the conditions of that time but the descent was even harder! The young priest was criticized and cursed for daring to climb the sacred mountain to see the remains of Noah's Ark. He would have fallen a victim of blind fanaticism had he not managed to escape to the University of Dorpat. After graduating from the university he rejected the brilliant career open to him, vowed to serve his people and, full of optimistic hope and plans, returned home.

Here he came into collision with clerical obscurantism. "Do you wish to give orders to me, faithless one? You may only confuse the minds of innocent people but it is not your task to educate them". This was how the reactionary Catholicos of the Holy See, Hovhannes Karbetsi, replied to Abovian's request to open a school for Armenian children.

Later, he was not only continually persecuted by

obscurantists but also harassed by narrow-minded tsarist officials who succeeded in getting rid of him at the age of forty-three.

Abovian came out of his Yerevan house close to his school in the early morning of April 2, 1848, and nobody ever saw him again.

No one knows whether he went up Mt. Ararat to find eternal peace in its pure snows or whether he was drowned in he River Hrazdan. Or, whether, as legend has it, he was driven away in a black coach to Siberia.

I think that the latter is most probable. One day the Siberian snows will reveal his traces...

But the fact remains that he vanished without leaving a tomb, and stony Armenia was again unable to lay a stone on the grave of one of her most beloved sons...!

Whereas it is definitely known that he was born, no one can prove that he died!

He shares the happy fate of the immortals whose lives do not span between the dates of birth and death...

> It's all too futile to search for a tomb,
> And to think of things already amiss...
> Whether he was dragged, drowned in Zangu,
> Or killed on his way to Mount Massis...
>
> Whether in the dark a foe shot him dead,
> Or the plotter's cart pulled him to his grave...
> It's hopeless a thing to be so upset,
> When he, Abovian... is alive and safe.

18—Seven songs about Armenia

Searching for death-roads is just to faddle.
There is only one similarity...
We know he was born, and had his cradle,
But no grave to mark his mortality...

Believe me, my friends, if you want to test,
Look at the life-road Abovian had crossed,
Here is the cradle which rocked him to rest,
His *Wounds of Armenia* — dear to us most...

Here is, standing high, Mount Ararat,
Like a memorial to his name well-known...
There is everything making him all great,
Everything, except...
                    his own grave-stone.

And why should we span so glorious a life,
Between the cradle and a sepulcher...?
To be born and keep constantly alive...!
It's a happy lot all would like to share...!

Although Abovian saw and sung the praises of one
"whole" Russia, he instinctively felt that there were in
fact two Russias — the Russia of Pushkin, whom he
adored and translated into Armenian, and that of Bulgar-
in, whom he once called on obsurantist during an ar-
gument at Dorpat.

... Mikael Nalbandian, a younger writer friend of
Abovian, was more fortunate, if one may use this word
in connection with an Armenian writer of the past, and,

more specifically, a talented writer and a man of principle.

He was quick to understand, and not instinctively, but consciously that there were two Russias — the Russia of Chernishevsky and Herzen and that of the tsars.

Publishing fiery books and passionate articles in the Moscow journal, *Hyussisapail* ("Northern Lights"), and later, engaging in revolutionary activities with Herzen, Chernishevsky and Ogariev in Russia and then in London, Nalbandian struggled whole-heartedly against autocracy in the name of the freedom and equality of nations. He was later imprisoned with Chernishevsky in Petropavlovsk fortress (their cells were adjacent) and he died in exile in Kamishin at the age of thirty-seven...

Nalbandian was the first revolutionary and poet-spokesman in our new literature.

O, Lyre, speak no more, spare me of your frauds...
And you Apollo, take it back from me...
Give it to someone who would willingly
Devote all his life to the girl he lauds...

I'll bring myself out without a lyre,
To speak openly with words hot as fire,
To cry all aloud, protest and defy,
And bitterly fight the forces of lie...

What's the use of lyre seeking love and fun?
The brave fighter needs the sword and the gun,
To strike at the foe with blood and with fire...
This is what, indeed, we shou'd all desire...!

And even at a time when Armenia was heaving under the yoke of the Turkish Sultans and lived in constant fear of plunders and massacres, and our literature naturally had a marked national colouring, Nalbandian, ever faithful to his lofty universal ideals, wrote: "So far man has not reached the point of being able to act under his natural name of man without the help of supplementary and official titles. So far there has been no *man* on earth, there have only been nations..."

And further on: "When a man appears in a nation, he does not give himself a name when he calls himself English, German, etc., we can only accept this phenomenon as a fact".

These words were written in the 19th century, but they do not sound as if they were from the distant past, but, on the contrary, from the bright horizons of the distant future.

Although Nalbandian had a short life, which was full of suffering, we were quite right in calling him fortunate. For there is surely no greater happiness for a noble-hearted man of principle than to suffer and die for the sake of his convictions.

Nalbandian was consciously ready to suffer and to die ever since he announced his credo to the world in his famous "In a Couple of Lines": "We have willingly dedicated ourselves to defend the rights of the common people... Staunchly defending these violated rights... is the sole aim and purpose of our life... And to achieve that aim we are not stopped by prisons or exile and we will serve it

not only with words and the pen but also with weapons and blood, if we are ever worthy enough to take up arms and consecrate the freedom we have been preaching with our own blood..."

The greatest of all contemporary Armenian poets is undoubtedly Hovhannes Toumanian. He is well and truly a classical poet who is read by both young and old, peasants and intellectuals.

To call Toumanian simply a poet of genius is too little: he is *great* — as great and *indispensable* as our daily bread.

From early childhood to a ripe old age every Armenian is accompanied by Toumanian's poems, verses, stories, articles, fables and skilful interpretations of folklore. One of their first books in childhood is "The Dog and the Cat" and one of their last, "Quatrains", "Farewell to Sirius" and "Requiem".

Toumanian writes in such a way as though it is not he writing but it is the mountains and gorges, the past and present of Armenia, the sorrow of Armenians and their bright faith in the future.

His characteristic poem "In the Armenian Mountains" condenses the very essence of the history of the Armenian people...

> For centuries-long we go up the height
> Through that endless gloom,
> Through that hopeless doom,
> With this path of ours in the pitch-black night,
> In these robust mounts,
> These Armenian mounts!

We carry with us our ancient wealth,
Immeasurably strong,
That for ages long,
Our soul has borne out of its depth,
In these lofty mounts,
These Armenian mounts...!

So numerous times we suffered the ban
Of the desert foes,
In succeeding rows,
That split our whole noble caravan,
In these bloody mounts,
These Armenian mounts...!

And this caravan almost scared to death,
Ravaged, robbed and pierced,
But holding its fist,
Still goes on to march with its immense wealth,
In these mournful mounts,
These Armenian mounts...!

We have now turned our craving eyes,
To the distant far,
To that northern star,
Anxious as to when will the bright dawn rise,
In these verdant mounts,
These Armenian mounts...!

... Avetik Issahakian, Toumanian's friend, is a poet of
intricate temperament embodying not only "the sorrow
of the Armenian people, but also "world sorrow", the grief
and anger of mankind, which the poet passionately ex-

pressed in his famous poem "Abu-Lala Mahari", subsequently translated into many languages.

The son of an Armenian peasant, Issahakian travelled the world over, studied in Russia, Germany and Switzerland and lived for a long time in France and Italy. He was familiar with all religions and teachings — from Buddah and Conficius, to Christ, Lao-Tsze, Nietzsche, Schopenhauer to Marx and Lenin and this complex fusion of human thoughts and emotions were expressed in his lucid, simple songs. He began his life under the light of the oil-lamp and ended it under the radio signals of the first rockets.

Issahakian's poems, especially his "Songs of an Exile", poems about love and nature, have been praised by many eminent 20th century poets and Alexander Blok, who in 1915 translated his verses into Russian, called him one of the best poets of the turn of the 20th century.

Issahakian's lyrical verses are so deeply rooted in the heart of the Armenian people that almost all of them are sung and most of these songs have been composed anonymously by peasants and artisans...

Issahakian is a master of wise lyrical miniatures which one remembers for the rest of one's life...

> Where is that stone,
> That stone of mine,
> Which is to be
> My future shrine...

Roaming the world,
Just all alone,
Have I not mourned,
On that same stone...?

His small verse written in Ravenna and dedicated to Mount Ararat is perhaps the best of all the verses dedicated to the eternal mountain.

Ages as though in seconds came,
Touched the grey crest of Ararat,
And passed by...!

Swords of lightnings in star numbers,
Crashed on its white diamond core,
And passed by...!

Panic-stricken generations,
Just gazed in awe at its bright top,
And passed by...!

It's now your turn; you too, now,
Stare at its high and lordly brow,
And pass by...!

... Now let us turn to Daniel Varuzhan and Siamanto, eminent poets of Western Armenia at the turn of the century, who were savagely murdered in 1915 by the Turkish butchers.

Varuzhan was an astonishing poet and one of our greatest, not only because of his truly fine but also because of his amazingly harmonious versatile nature.

Varuzhan wrote about almost everything from the

first "Tremors" of youth down to the tragic "Heart of the Nation", bold "Workers' Songs" and masterpieces of Armenian poetry, which could compete with the best works of world poetry, such as the brilliant "Heathen Songs", the poem "The Concubine" and the tenderly simple "Song of Bread".

Whatever subject a real poet should write on, be it the most intimate personal feelings, or something very trifling, it is always of interest because it is an expression of his "self" which embodies the whole world.

This idea had been very wittingly expressed by the Russian poet Batyushkov: "Why do we enjoy reading Candemir's books? Because he writes *about himself!* And why do we dislike reading Shalikov's books? Because he writes *about himself!*

That is, the confessions of a *real poet,* who can't fail to be also a great person and citizen, makes interesting reading.

His soul is similar to a "super-saturated solution" in chemistry in which any substance at once becomes coated with fine crystals and turns into a wonderful work of art.

On the other hand, even the "gold" of the most splendid theme, when plunged into the watery solution of an empty and trivial soul, becomes a mundane fact of man's daily life and fails as poetry.

What could be more trivial then having a small insect suddenly fall into one's eye?

However, Varuzhan has created one of his best verses on this trifling subject:

You were spreed by Spring, too dizzy to see
Falling in my eye, as into a sea!
And swinging in search of a safety shore,
You just spoiled your wings on its glassy core...!

... Then, as a cloud, my eye-lid engulfed you,
And my pup within, gleaming bright, was due
To become your grave!
                    And the very tear,
Which nearly killed you, had to mourn you, dear!
Yours was death atoned for your curious sin,
And mine — just to weep, though never foreseen...!

Ever since the Middle Ages many Armenian poets have extolled love, which was, however, for the most part platonic (particularly in the 18th-19th centuries literature).

Varuzhan was the first to introduce a real-live woman into modern Armenian poetry and to extol physical beauty and passion ("Eastern Baths") "The Concubine", "O, Lalageh", and many others).

... The history of our people's spiritual life has from the very start been a history of the worship of light, wisdom, nobility and goodness.

"Joyful Light" and "Morning Light" are the titles of songs we have sung for hundreds of years now.

Every day we greet one another with the words "Good Light" ("Good morning"), and "May your eyes be filled with Light" (Congratulations). Varuzhan continues this eternal theme in his poem "I Go Towards The Spring of Light".

But heading towards the spring of light, our people were again brutally attacked by the spirit of darkness:

> ... And over there, in the plane,
> Life is slaughtered,
> As the idea — in the brain...

And Varuzhan, who was born for light and beauty, sung the praises of his nation that had been "betrayed by the centuries but allowed by eternity", extolling its wounds and rebellious nature, condemned the new murderers of Light, and finally fell their victim at the age of thirty...

He was endowed with a vivid imagination, but the only thing he could not imagine was that he and his writer friend Siamanto, who extolled the man-god in verse would be killed in a desert ravine by a barbarian with blood-shot eyes who smashed their heads with stones...!

If Varuzhan's corpse were found, it could be mourned with the words of his poem:

> This is the night of triumph great and glorious!
>   Bride, have the lamp filled with oil...
> My warrior son is coming back victorious,
>   Bride, trim the wick churned and coil...
>
> A cart did stop near the door, by the well...
>   Bride, kindle it like a torch...
> It is my son with his forehead wreathed and swell...
>   Bride, bring the lamp to the porch...
>
> But why... as though there's blood and woe in the cart...
>   Bride, stretch your lamp here about...

> My hero son is deadly hit in the heart...!
> Oh, Bride, your light, blow it out...!

From a young age Siamanto, Varuzhan's older writer friend had witnessed nothing but massacres, plunders and persecutions, and had been writing about these horrors.

He was only sixteen when the Armenian massacres of 1895-96 began in Constantinople and the provinces.

It would have been natural for a youth of sixteen to have seen only the attractive sides of life, such as nature, spring, love and dreams!

However, Siamanto only saw massacres and fires, and only one colour of all the dazzling ones in the world — that of blood...

He was born to be the lyrical echo of his Armenian village, but instead he became a chronicler of horrors and sufferings of crimes, or as he put it, "the pale youth offered as a sacrifice".

Whereas Armenian poets living in exile for centuries pined for home, for Siamanto home did not exist: it had been destroyed and Siamanto's greatest dream was to be able at least to hold a handful of ash from his home in his hour of death...

> Alas: You were just as splendid as a palace,
> And I, standing on top of your white roofs,
> With the hope of nights in the flickering stars,
> I used to hear the wild flow of the Euphrates...
>
> I almost wept seeing your walls
> Fall in ruins one by one...

It was a day of fright, a bloody day,
For the flowers bordering you...

... My native land, do believe me, after my death,
My soul, rising from the ashes of your ruins,
Will visit you, as tenderly as an exiled dove,
To shed its tears and mournful songs...

And yet tell me, who is to bring, who is to bring,
A handful of your sacred ash,
To scatter it over my grave,
And mix it up with that of mine — your poet dear?

My native home, who is to bring just a handful
Of your own ash to mix it up with that of mine,
Out of your past, out of your woes and memory,
Just a handful, to scatter it... over my heart...?

Siamanto died knowing that "the dawn of justice is still hopelessly far off", and he angrily exclaimed to the indifferent world:

O, human justice,
Let me spit you in the face...!

However, with his sensible ear of a poet he already sensed the "red news" coming to his country and people, soon to be hailed by Vahan Terian and Yeghisheh Charents...

But before passing on to Vahan Terian and Yeghisheh Charents, let us trace the history of the Armenian alphabet up to the recent past, which marked the beginning of the Golden Age of our lieterature, culture and science.

It's quite impossible to count the innumerable treasures of our age-old culture! But at the same time one shouldn't forget that the people who created this immensely rich culture, were not always able to make use of it.

Everybody knows that even the letters created by Mesrop Mashtots were compelled to wander from place to place for 1600 years before reaching their own people!

And over the centuries up to a couple of decades ago some of our people were still unable to sign their names and instead stamped their finger-prints on the paper, or drew a cross, as if symbolizing the obscurity and misery in which our people had suffered for so many centuries.

Even at the turn of the twentieth century, many writers dreamed about the day when Armenian peasants would read their works.

Only one hundred years ago Khachatur Abovian dreamed with little real hope of having a hundred children at his school.

He could never have imagined that the day would come when there would be 1600 schools, colleges and institutes in Armenia at which over a third of the population would be studying.

Neither could he have imagined that twenty-six million books would be stored in the libraries of Armenia and if everyone in the country, including the very young and old, were to turn up at the libraries at the same time, there would still be over ten books for each person!

What would be the reaction of a French or English diplomat of the past if he were told that the number of students at higher educational institutions in Armenia today long ago exceeded that of France and England (of course, in proportion to the over-all population).

The students at these secondary and higher education establishments are not only from Armenia but also from many Soviet and foreign cities.

... According to statistics, in 1828 Yerevan had a population of 11,563!

However, statistical data give hardly any information about the real population, about the poor, honest Armenian workers,craftsmen and gardeners who were making our country a better place to live in.

On the other hand, we learn for a fact that in 1828 Yerevan was inhabited by "four khans, fifty beks... thirty-nine seids, three dervishes...

I do not know how many of these "eminent" people were literate but one can't help laughing when one reads of them in Yerevan today which is literally bursting at the seams because of the tremendous number of educated people, and where it is becoming hard to find people who left school at fifteen.

And nowadays even in the "remotest" villages of Armenia you'll find at least 20-30 teachers (with higher education), agriculturists, doctors and other specialists.

Schools, colleges, libraries, universities... Not long ago, however, Armenians had to go to Leipzig and Geneva, Paris and London to receive a higher aducation... Now young people from many countries of the world come to Yerevan for that same reason!

19—Seven songs about Armenia

And what about the Armenian Academy of Sciences? For centuries our talented scientists of the past, mathematicians, doctors, astronomers and philologists dreamed of having one such centre.

... In medieval Armenia many universities and academies existed at various periods such as the academy of Hovhannes Vorotnetsi, the Gladzor University, the school of philosopher Grigor Tatevatsi and the academy of Grigor Magistros in Kecharis.

But there had never been and never could have been a single academy of sciences for the whole country.

All the schools and academies mentioned above were mainly interested in philology and theology.

Here is what our friend Hakop the scribe wrote about the university of Hovhan Vorotnetsi in 1386: "And we studied with the patronage of His Holiness and Grace Archbishop of Armenia Hovhan Vorotnetsi at his university which shone like a sun at that obscure, troubled time. He gathered orphans and homeless people from near and far, taught them and worked wonders, turning some into teachers and priests, others into musicians, philosophers, painters and clerks".

The following is about Tovma Metsopetsi who was educated at Tatev University: "He acquired knowledge of twelve branches of philosophical science: 1) Natural science; 2) Pedagogy; 3) Theology; 4) Ethics; 5) Economics; 6) Politics; 7) Mathematics; 8) Music; 9) Geometry; 10) Astronomy; 11) Seven literary works on various questions of philosophic rhetorics, (such as *Grammar* by

Dionysius Thrax, *Book of Definitions* by David Anhaght, *Prologue* by Porphyry, the interpretation of the "Categories" by Aristotle, the works by Pseudo-Aristotle and others; 12) The Bible, the Gospels and literary works of 50 historians".

What an astonishingly high level of education for that time and what an enviable knowledge of the various sciences and philosophical teachings! This helps to explain the seriousness and depth of the outlooks of medieval Armenian historians, philosophers and scientists, and the unusual abundance of translations of old scientific books into Armenian.

When speaking about the old Armenian scientific centres, one has to mention the famous congregation of Mkhitarists in Venice!

Convinced after many futile attempts that it was impossible to recreate the medieval scientific centres or set-up new ones in Armenia, Armenian progressive historians and scholars, headed by Mkhitar Sebastatsi in 1717 founded a large scientific research centre on the Island of St. Lazarus near Venice, which still functions with its famous subsidiary branch in Vienna and puts out scientific works and journals.

The Mkhitarist friars were the first Armenian encyclopedists — it was they who first produced a scientific edition of the old Armenian manuscripts and carefully studied all Armenia's ancient architectural monuments and became the first Armenian encyclopedists. The Mkhitarist friars were so devoted to their work that many of them, who

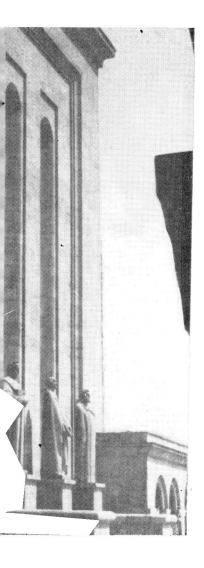

The Institute of ancient manuscripts, the Matenadaran...

had never been to Armenia, such as Ghevond Alishan, a poet and a linguist, described each of its towns and villages, springs and graves, stones and bushes in such detail only on the basis of what they had read, that one cannot help admiring them.

As for their fantastic industriousness each of them did as much work on his own as that of a whole scientific research institute.

The journals, books, dictionaries and text-books sent from the island of St. Lazarus to Armenia and then the teachers who arrived from there reanimated Armenia's cultural life which had become deadened under foreign repression, and revived traditions of the past.

Incidentally, it was on the Island of St. Lazarus that the first foreign specialists on Armenia became interested in Armenian history, language and culture of Armenia. Their noble work was later carried on by Meillet, Maclair, Hubschmann, Markwart, Dulorien, Brosset, and at present by Frederik Feidin, Charles Dawsett, Thomson, Vlad Benatsianu, Triarsky, Smushkevich, Yaromir Edlichka, Lyudmilla Motalova, Gerard Harrid, Bolonesy, Schuts, Pisovich, Benvenist, Robert Godell and Lung, to name but a few.

It was also there on the Island of St. Lazarus that Byron, enchanted by Armenia and Armenian culture, spent many months studying them and even wrote a preface for the Mkhitarist Armenian-English dictionary.

Visitors to the Island of St. Lazarus may still see

Byron's study, the oak tree he planted and the bench on which he sat and composed poetry.

...Yes, there were universities and academies in medieval Armenia but as Armenia had no statehood, there couldn't be a unified academic centre.

What had been impossible to do for centuries, was done by our people at the most dificult time for the country — during the Great Patriotic War...

As shells roared in the Caucasian mountains, the Armenian branch of the USSR Academy of Sciences was inaugurated in Yerevan and then we saw our first president, Hovsep Orbeli, a great academic wise and charming man whose venerable face resmebled that of a medieval Armenian miniature.

The renowned Armenian philologists Hrachya Adjarian, Manuk Apeghian, Hakop Manandian, Stepanos Malkhasian, Grigor Ghapantsian and many others were fortunate enough to become the founding members of our Academy.

At present there are more then 12,000 researchers and over 4000 scientists at scientific research institutions of the Academy of Sciences of Armenia. Among them are world-famous scientists such as Victor Hambartsumian, Artyom Alikhanian, Sergei Mergelian, Mkhitar Cherbashian, Abgar Hovhannisian and Suren Yeremian.

Our Academy of Sciences has been greatly assisted for many years by outstanding scientists such as Levon Orbeli, Ezras Hasratian, Khachatur Koshtoyants, Issahak Alikhanian, Norair Sisakian, Nikolai Tokarsky, Boris Piotrovsky and many other Russian scientists.

Mount Aragats, which used to be famous only for its picturesque beauty, is now a scientific centre and closely surveilled by scientists...

The physicists, specialists of cosmic radiation and astrophysics of many countries who have never been to Armenia, are well acquainted with the names of the villages Byurakan and Amberd which are connected with many discoveries and bold hypotheses in these spheres. Scientific symposiums and congresses of world significance are held here, too.

It was here on the slopes of Mt. Aragats that the Alikhanian brothers carried out experiments in cosmic radiation, that Victor Hambartsumian, one of the sons of our people scattered all over the world like a constellation, proved the theory that stars and planets are not created once and forever but are constantly being created.

If one wanted to find out what we have inherited most from the remote past, one wouldn't have to think for very long. Armenia has always cherished the written word and literature most dearly.

Although many things in our lives today were invented in the last few decades or are like tiny streams trickling down to us from the past, literature and culture reached us in the form of an overflowing river, a rich store of priceless cultural treasures.

There is nothing more difficult and more honourable than being an Armenian writer, a representative of a literature which has such rich traditions.

It is difficult because one not only has to compete with

all the best that has been inherited from the past and be worthy of it, but one also has to add something original and new to it.

Our modern Armenian literature, however, has not only said something new of its own: it has also created classic literary works which are worthy of standing side by side with the best works of the past.

Among those who have added something original and new to our literature was Vahan Terian, one of the subtlest Armenian poets of the 20th century.

His poetry and life were similar to an avenue strewn with sad autumn leaves which finally led him to Lenin at Smolny to sing the praises of the red banner of the October Revolution.

A year before his death, in 1919, when he was only thrity four, Vahan Terian wrote: "Why didn't I die when I was young?"

Maybe not in other respects, but in this respect fate was "generous" with Armenian poets; Terian died at the age of thirty five, as Misak Metsarents at the age of 22 and the young genius Petros Dourian at twenty!

Before Vahan Terian, Eastern Armenian poetry mostly came from the country.

As I have already mentioned, the subject, main character and author of a book were all peasants and this could not help influence our literature.

Terian was one of the first to write about the town, its pavements and night lights, students, tramps, emotions and thoughts of town intellectuals; his love and struggle with new poetic forms and means.

Unlike many of his predecessors, Terian confessed rather than preached, trustingly revealed his innermost secrets rather than told stories or described, created a certain state of mind and mood rather than invented a fascinating image or line; gently won the reader over rather than forcing him to listen.

Terian wrote little but in such a way that there is almost no need to prepare his selected works. Each is unique and selected in its own right from his *Dreams of Twilight* down to the tragic but optimistic cycle of verses *Land of Nairi.*

Throughout our stormy history at the outset of each new war and calamity our poets have anxiously wondered whether the end was near. Terian also asked this age-old question:

> Am I to be the last poet,
> The last poet of my country?
> Or, is it death coming so great,
> To shroud you my bright Nairy...?
>
> I dream of you in colours bright,
> In a country foreign and grey...
> And when speaking your noble tongue,
> It seems to me as if I pray...
>
> I call on you, frightened, upset,—
> Cheer up in hope, dreamy Nairy...
> Am I to be the last poet,
> The last poet of my country...?

Two years after he asked this question, the tragedy of 1915 occurred. However, convinced of the miraculous revival of his people, Terian answered this question himself in another verse:

As that noble Mount heaps up all snow-falls,
We are accustomed to endure all blows...
But take Babylon with its iron fist,
Now lies in ruins, in dust and in mist...
Assyria came next, struck and broke its hand,
And lies dead and dry as a barren land...
...Pyramids will fall and turn into dust,
But you have to shine, my land, as you must!
Barbarians will come and perish in vain,
Our noble tongue will always remain...

Endowed with magic talent and charm, Terian founded a literary school but in the last years of his life he was always dissatisfied with his verses and tried to express the new revolutionary breath in the world. He changed his harmonious-sounding verses into blank verse and adopted a conversational style which was an altogether new trend for him.

Red banner of freedom,
I glorify thee...!
My poor gloomy soul
Has brightened again,
Rising and soaring as a wild petrel
Amidst wind and gale...!

This was already what Yeghisheh Charents would later do, and it was by no mere chance that Charents was the poet to take the immortal torch of Armenian poetry from Terian's hands.

Yeghisheh Charents!

He is the golden bridge linking Armenian classical poetry with that of our revived Armenia, a poet who encaptured all the best features of age-old Armenian poetry, and at the same time created the best modern poetry.

Charents was not simply a poet: his poetry was the main artery of our poetry and his books were *The Guide-Line to Books,* as one of his books was entitled.

Like Boileau, he left us his *Ars Poetica* paving the way for the poets to come after him and gave them the golden key to many new themes of the future.

His literary works are a biography of our country, starting with the *Dantesque Legend* engendered in the Genocide and World War I, the stormy poems of *Soma* and *The Frantic Masses* down to the brilliant poetic novel *Land of Nairi,* and *A Poem to All* and *The Epic Dawn* heralding the birth of the Soviet Armenian classical poetry, and *The Guide-Line to Books,* his last work in which he crystallized all the history of our people.

Charents was a great prophet. Who else in 1918 could have foreseen and picked up the radio signals of the rockets and spaceships of today while eulogizing the naked frantic crowds struggling for the revolution?

> Within their tight muscles and fists
> Lies the full strength of the damp earth...
> And at their will — heavenly stars
> And suns may change their path and worth...

> They may, at will, be as mindful
> As to throw suns into the skies...
> And if they want — they'll mark and pull
> The suns down back from the skies...
>
> What will they not do and achieve,
> If they want to — the frantic throngs...!

A staunch fighter and conscientious citizen, Charents not only eulogized all the best of his age, he also fiercely waged war against everything that was wicked, false, base and vicious, whether it be a "red Philistine", a political demagogue and slanderer or the impending danger of the personality cult.

He waged a noble and savage struggle for inner content against exterior appearance, for the *idea* against the form; for meaning against hackneyed words, for lines written with Blood against those written with cheap ink.

Charents, the great revolutionary poet, has left behind his sacred testament as a poet and citizen of high principle and integrity in word and in deed, life and death.

Charents, the great poet of his people and revolution, was only forty when the enemies of that same people and revolution accelerated his immortality, when he still had so many things to tell us. He was turned into bronze and marble when the blood flowing through his veins was still warm!

"He has departed like the dead of thousands of years ago", his relatives sadly say of the deceased.

"He has departed like the immortals of thousands of years ago", one might proudly say of Yeghisheh Charents who is now ranked on a par with Narekatsi, Kuchak, Toumanian and Terian.

"Like...? No, no...!

Just as when he was here on earth, there, too, he has taken up his own unique place. Among the immortals!

A new contribution to Armenian poetry was also made by Avetik Issahakian who returned to his homeland in 1936, and added new literary works such as *Sasma Mher* (Mher of Sassoun), *Bingyol* and *War Cry* to his wonderful early ones.

A new contribution was also made by Derenik Demirdjian, a most talented writer. His historical novel *Vardanank* published during the Great Patriotic War accomplished as much as several divisions. His death unfortunately prevented him from reviving the image of Mesrop Mashtots sixteen centuries after the latter's death...

Another who deserves mention is Stepan Zorian, the first to depict an Armenian woman-revolutionary. He described newly revived Armenia in *The White City* and created the historical novels *King Pap* and *The Armenian Fortress*.

With the magic force of his talent Axel Bakunts recreated *The Gorge Lost in Darkness* and brought it into the light. He did not manage to complete his novel *Khachatur Abovian,* one of the best in Soviet Armenian literature.

A new contribution was also made by Nairi Zarian with his stormy *Voice of the Homeland* and immortal *Ara the Beautiful;* by Hovhannes Shiraz, the inimitable lyrical poet of nature and motherly love with his *Biblical* cycle; by Paruir Sevak, my close friend who died prematurely, with his *"Unsilenced Bell-Tower* and unique poems. And finally new contributions are now being made by the talented and celebrated poets whose voice is that of our new Armenia resounding all over the world.

Many of their verses have been put to music and are now being sung the world over.

Let us listen to one of these songs which is about song itself...

THE SONG
OF SONGS

As an old song goes: "God save the Armenian people..." Not the tsar or the King but the people — the workers, one and all.

It would be hard to find an Armenian who hasn't sung or heard the song *Kroonk* (Crane) about an exile longing for his homeland:

Kroonk, where d'you come from? Let me hear your voice
For some news in which I could well rejoice.
Hold on, ere you fly, you've no other choice.
Haven't you some news from my native land...?

I have left behind my orchard and home,
I awefully sigh wherever I roam...
Kroonk, stop a bit, before you fly on...
Havn't you some news from my native land...?

... Things go always slow, my sorrow is deep,
I spend day and night in no rest and sleep,
It's an exile's lot to mourn and to weep...
Haven't you some news from my native land...?

No more can I dream of a quiet day.
I seem I'm in fire as a spitted prey.
Missing my dear ones is my only care.
Haven't you some news from my native land...?

Having left Baghdad, you're flying away...
I have a short note written in dismay.
Take it to my folks just there, on your way...
Haven't you some news from my native land....

I have informed them that since I came here,
I have never had a sole day of cheer,
I have missed them all, just year after year,
Haven't you some news from my native land....

Autumn has drawn near, you're anxious to fly.
In hundreds of flocks you started to fly...
I asked for some news, you gave no reply...
Kroonk, then be off out of my land...!

The fate of our people is, as it were, condensed in this song. For centuries it has been sung in Armenia so often that it has become our "unofficial" national anthem — an anthem filled with nostalgia and sorrow. Plagued by wars and never-ending disasters, the people left their homes and, like the crane, moved to foreign lands. And, like the crane, too, their songs and arts wandered from country to country.

Their songs and arts were subjected to fire and the sword both in their own land and in exile, but they withstood them and have survived to this day

But have they really? Yes, of course, at least some of

them, a mere handful of the countless treasures, a few carved stones from a devastated temple, a few tattered feathers from the immortal legendary fire-bird, a few muted notes from the enchanting hymns, and a few songs have been passed down to us by word of mouth by peasants and minstrels.

Who could count the number of pagan temples, like that of Garni which were subject to fire and the sword and destroyed with the coming of Christianity!

Who could count the number of works like Vahagn's Birth and the pagan legends about Ara the Beautiful, Artashess, Artavazd and Tigran the Great which were burned on the fires of Christian excommunication and only the smoke of the sumptuous feast of Navasard[1] has reached us.

As the old song Memories of King Artashess goes:

> Who'd give me back the chimney smoke,
> And the morning of Navasard...
> The running deer,
> And speeding elks,
> While we bugled,
> And beat the drums, .
> As in those days of reigning kings...?

Who could count how many "sinful" minstrels were put to death, how many lyres and lutes smashed, how many songs stifled, how many dancers tortured like Na-

---

[1] Navasard — first month of the old Armenian calendar.

zenik in the second century B.C. about whom all we know is that "she was very beautiful and her hands sung".

No one will ever find the victims burned by the first Christian fanatics, in the fires which blazed over the mountains and valleys; the statues of heathen gods of which only one has survived — that of the goddess Anahit which is now in the British Museum! And what about the Christian fanatics, in the fires which blazed over the melodies? Although they existed secretly it wasn't easy for them to be passed on by word of mouth for two or three thousand years without being lost or deformed. Even if their words were recorded later on, how was it possible for the melody to be passed on to us?

Just as no one now could break the silence of the manuscripts of the Matenadaran which were petrified by the horrors they suffered, no one, not even our great composer Komitas, who found all the true sources of our melodies, has succeeded in deciphering the Armenian notes which abound between the lines of the old folk songs and religious hymns.

These songs are like sea-waves which have turned to stone before reaching us on the shore and we will never be able to hear their sounds.

It is impossible to imagine how great our treasures were judging by the handful of priceless works which have survived.

Nevertheless, a lot has survived.

We have clear traces of the great civilization of Mokhrablur and Metsamor, remains of the Erebuni Fortress

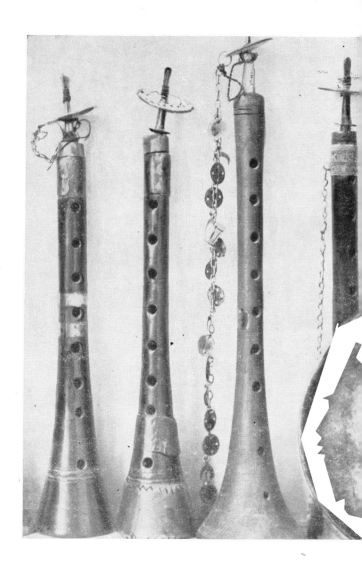

and the fortress town of Karmir Blur, the Temple of Garni
and its unique mosaics, the bronze head of the Goddess
Anahit and the bas-reliefs of the Temple of Akhtamar
found at Garni, the ivory flute over two thousand years
old and the theatrical stone mask from Artashat.

We have the medieval "mystery" plays veiled with
religious themes; the pictures and masks used by actors
and even examples of ancient musical instruments...

We are truly fortunate to have our amazing miniatures
which were influenced by Byzantine Miniatures but often
excelled them. Well before the Italian Renaissance and
Giotto they had depth and perspective.

And the darker the gloom of the Middle Ages, the richer
and more luxurious the colours of our miniatures became.
Roaming across Armenia, talented Sarkis Pitsak, Tserun
Tsakhkogh, and the genius Toros Roslin by name, and an
unknown magic painter from Nor Djugha gradually imbibed the azure hues of the Armenian sky and the green-
ness of the fields of the Armenian land, blended with
cochineal and pure gold and with their brushes gave them
immortal life in such a way that even today they are so
fresh, they look as if they were painted yesterday.

Although many Armenian folk songs and religious
hymns have been lost in eternal silence, we have parts of
the Holy Mass, a few melodies of *The Dare-Devils of
Sassoun,* a hymn composed by Komitas, a 7th century
catholicos, *The Devout Persons,* a wonderful song by the
medieval poet Baghdassar Dpir *Wake up, my Dear One,*
other secular medieval songs, marvellous liturgies and

songs and melodies by Naghash Hovnatan and Sayat-Nova...

And, finally, we have our most precious treasures — our folk songs which reached us like spring floods and were cleansed of all their impurities by Komitas and converted into an eternal source which is now frequently used by Armenian and foreign composers.

And what are Armenian songs about? They are lullabies, work songs, love, exile and pilgrim songs, humourous songs and elegies.

Many songs are, of course, about exile but even more are about peace!

Our people, who have suffered in endless wars, have always dreamed about peace and freedom and expressed their secret thoughts in songs.

"Grant the world peace and the people freedom" is the refrain in one of the oldest songs still sung and it is hard to believe that it was not written recently but in the 5th century.

The songs about peace prevail but the basic plea in all our songs is to help the Armenian people exist.

Just imagine the terrible conditions the talented creative people of Armenia were put in when they had to expend most of their talent and skill on finding ways and of staying alive and not always succeeded.

As one of our old hymn goes: "God save the Armenian people" not the tsar, king or heroes but the whole working people.

When the spring of Armenian songs abounded in the

Armenian mountains, and the colours in Armenian paintings dazzled the eye, Armenian artists, who had drunk from this source and collected these colours and were exiled and persecuted like most of our people, displayed their brilliant talent in foreign theatres and embellished foreign towns with their sculptures, conservatories and art exhibitions, wrote books in foreign languages and the like...

Petros Adamian, the great Shakespearian actor, performed in foreign theatres bearing the traditions of our two thousand-year-old theatre.

Tigran Chukhadjian, the renowned composer, staged his opera "Karineh" in Constantinople, thus laying the foundations of the Turkish musical theatre.

Arab audiences in Egypt were held spellbound by the Armenian actress Siranush (who later died in an Egyptian hospital) acting the title role of Hamlet in Armenian. In Paris the sculptor Ter-Marukian sculpted the splendid statue of Khachatur Abovian.

And the fate of the creative people who stayed in Armenia was hard and sometimes tragic.

In one single night — that of April 24, 1915,— almost all the famous public figures, statesmen, scientists, writers, artists, musicians, and actors of Western Armenia were arrested and killed and the great composer Komitas was driven insane by the atrocities...

> The road was long, as were the thoughts
> Lingering on along that road...

One might think of staging some halts,
But not in thoughts, strangling the throat...

On walked the group of Armenians,
And among them a "vanakan",[*]
With eyes frozen, void of brilliance,
Murmuring low a "sharakan"...[**]

He sang and thought in dreadful fears...
"Even the stone would break as if...
Euphrates flows in woeful tears...
Mount Nemrut darkens in grief...

A dying land is what they left,
And a handful of mourners sad...
Who would think of being so cleft,
As to bury all with the dead...?

He sang and thought...
                    That immense pain
Was not a cowl to brush away...
No thought could bear its heavy strain,
No heart could stand its dreadful weight...

It grew so dull and deadly dark
And so savage around him,
It seemed as if the world lost mark,
And tumbled off beyond its brim...

The bloody Turk that night came drunk
And reported to Taleat...

---

[*] A clergyman
[**] A religious hymn

Rockwell Kent wrote that one
couldn't help marvelling the
kind of monuments...

"They were shot dead...
Only a monk,
Still on his way collapsed, went mad..."

It seemed as though the Armenian age-old song had been silenced forever and not a sound would be heard in Armenia except the crackling of conflagrations, the howling of winds, the shrieks of terror and the low chanting of psalms by insane Komitas.

But is it possible for a monster to defeat man, or the past to defeat the future?

"A people that does not wish to die, will never die! The precious drop of blood which is still flowing in the veins of Armenia will give birth to a new generation of heroes tomorrow!" — wrote Anatole France immediately after the Genocide of 1915, prophezing our revitalized Armenia of today.

Years later, Rockwell Kent, one of the greatest painters of modern times, wrote that you can't help marvelling, seeing in this tiny corner of the world the kind of monuments and people who may be the pride and joy of the whole world...!

Whereas for many centuries foreign pilgrims have been coming on pilgrimages to Armenia to see Mount Ararat where the legendary miracle of Noah's Ark took place, people nowadays come from all over the world to look at the *real* miracle that has taken place at the foot-hills of Mt. Ararat, whose life-giving breath has been instilled in our literature, music, painting and theatre...

Most theatre historians of the world know that two

thousand years ago the Armenian capital town of Artashat had its own theatre where plays by both Armenian and Greek playwrights were performed and that during one of these performances the head of the executed Roman general Crassus was brought onto the stage...

But they should also know that in 1920...

But let's first finish our story about Artashat in those far-off days when even Jesus Christ, the main character in the tragedy of Christianity which has been performed for twenty centuries now, had not yet been born.

So, two thousand years ago, at the theatre of Artashat the head of the executed Roman general, Marcus Crassus, was brought on to the stage. Yes, of that arrogant Crassus who had once crushed the famous rebellion of Spartacus and crucified the thousands of rebellious gladiators on both sides of the Appian Way. According to contemporary accounts, he would have crucified even more if he had had enough crosses.

At that time Roman legions were fighting in Mesopotamia against the allied forces of the Armenians and Parthians.

The Armenian King, Artavazd II, a dramatist and ardent lover of Hellenic culture and theatre, organized a great feast in his capital town of Artashat in honour of his Partian ally, King Vorotes I.

In order to strengthen and consolidate the Armeno-Parthian treaty of friendship, Artavazd II gave his sister in marriage to Prince Pakoor, the son of Vorotes.

That day the theatre of Artashat staged Euripides'

21—Seven songs about Armenia

drama, *The Bacchae* in which the main role was acted by Jason, the famous Greek tragedian.

In keeping with the role, Jason had to appear on the stage with the head of Pentheus slain by the Bacchae on his shield, and then recite his famous maniologue:

> As a sign of a lucky game,
> We are bringing home a deer,
> Just slaughtered in the mountains...

When Jason was getting ready to appear on the stage, a messenger of general Suren of the Parthians rushed into the theatre. He brought news of victory from the battlefield near the town of Carra, and the decapitated head of Crassus. Clever Jason seizing Crassus' head from the hands of the messenger, put it on the shield and ran onto the stage. The two allied kings and the audience hailed him with a thunderous ovation as he began reciting his monologue, erasing the boundaries between reality and fiction and giving the latter new meaning.

Incidentally bearing in mind the importance of the victory of the East over Rome at Carra, one may surmise that King Artavazd II was a producer as well as a dramatist that day: knowing of the victory, he purposely chose Euripides' play and acted out the scene with Crassus' head with Jason beforehand. Whatever really happened, one thing is clear: arrogont Crassus, who had sent Spartacus into the arena to be tortured, "reaped what he had sown" and turned into a dummy head on the Artashat stage.

This performance at Artashat, referred to as the "Armenian Carthage" by the Romans, was the first recorded play staged in Armenia. According to Plutarch, it took place on May 7th or 8th, 53 B.C.

However, the theatre existed in Armenia even earlier, during the reign of King Tigran the Great who, according to Plutarch, invited many Greek actors to the inauguration of the new theatre in his capital town of Tigranakert. These actors were later used by Lucullus in the victory celebrations on seizing the town.

The Hellenic theatre in Armenia prospered for about five hundred years, up to the 3rd-4th centuries A.D.

Later, from the 4th century onwards, militant Christianity destroyed the pagan arts and especially the theatre, which in medieval Armenia existed only in the form of mystery plays.

We know very little about the medieval Armenian theatre, axcept that the Church condemned the theatre as "pagan", "wicked" and "engendred by the Antichrist".

In such conditions, historians naturally could not write about the popular and minstrel theatres which performed "operatic-fairy-tales" and puppet shows.

Until recently (I saw them myself in Yerevan about forty years ago) itinerant minstrels on their own or in groups performed such "operatic-fairy-tales" in the squares and market places of our towns and villages.

After a long interval, in the 17th-18th centuries the Armenian theatre was again mentioned. It was now professionally organised in the Armenian colonies in Lvov,

Venice, and Yerevan and then in Tbilisi, Baku, Novy-Nakhidjevan, and Astrakhan, to name only a few.

The French traveller Chardin described in his travel notes how in 1664 he personally watched a play being performed in Yerevan.

The next well-known theatrical parformance was a play entitled *The Martyrdom of the Virgin St. Hripsimeh* staged by students of the Armenian school of Lvov in 1668. Subsequently, more and more about theatrical performances was recorded.

In the 19th and 20th centuries there were already eminent actors and talented Armenian theatre groups who performed a carefully selected repertoire including classical and national plays in and outside of Armenia.

Performances given by such outstanding actors as Mnakian, Petros Adamian, Siranush, Vahram Papazian, Hovhannes Abelian and many others were highly successful not only in Armenia but also in Russia, France, Italy, America, Turkey and Persia.

Thanks to these touring companies and actors, Shakespeare became deeply rooted in the hearts of Armenian people. In fact, he became so much part of them that a great many Armenian peasants naively considered that *Hamlet* and *Othello* were Armenian plays (this was undoubtedly also due to Hovhannes Masehian's excellent translations which sound so wonderful in Armenian. Even now you may meet very many small dark-eyed runny-nosed Hamlets, Laerts, Ophelias and Desdemonas in the most remote corners of Armenia.

I don't know if there are special Shakespeare centres and libraries in many countries but I do know for certain that there is one in Armenia, and they can only be organised by people who count Shakespeare as a fellow countryman and love him dearly.

The following incident is most typical of the love of our people for Shakespeare. During the Shakespeare Congress and Festival held in Yerevan in 1944, a lot of the foreign participants decided also to visit Etchmiadzin and Oshakan (during the war this area was prohibited and special permit was needed). On the way their cars were stopped by a sentry.

"Who are you? Show your permits",— the young Armenian border-guard ordered them.

"We're taking part in the Shakespeare Festival",— one of them replied,— if I'm not mistaken, Yuzovsky, a theatre critic.

"I see... Pass!" commanded the Armenian border-guard, accepting Shakespeare's name as a special permit.

Petros Adamian's interpretation of Hamlet is still remembered by many Armenian and Russian theatre critics. The Armenian actor Mnakian is rightly considered the founder of the theatre in Turkey and the tragedian actor Vahram Papazian, also brilliant in his own right, was one of the best actors of Shakespearian theatre, and a fine scholar of Shakespeare.

As ill fate would have it, the centres of Armenian culture were mostly founded outside Armenia in Constantinople, Baku, Tbilisi, Novy-Nakhichevan, Moscow, the

Crimea and elsewhere. It was there that Armenian theatrical companies operated and from there they set off on tours to their homeland. It was also there that outstanding dramatists such as Hakop Baronian, Gabriel Sundukian, Levon Shant and Shirvanzadeh lived and worked.

In present-day Armenia the theatre began to operate more or less regularly in Yerevan since 1828 after the liberation of Yerevan from Persia when Griboyedov's play *Woe from Wit* was staged for the first time at the Palace of the Persian Sardar.

The second oldest theatre in Armenia was that of Alexandropole (Leninakan), whose centenary was celebrated in 1965.

But however rich and old the history and traditions of the Armenian theatre were, future theatre critics will undoubtedly consider the year 1922 as an important landmark, for it was then that the first state theatre of Armenia was founded in Yerevan — the theatre, which opened with a performance of Sundukian's play *Pepo* and which proudly bears his name.

It was soon followed by a touring theatre named after Hamo Kazarian and then by many others, such as the workers' theatre, opera, Russian, Kurdish, Azerbaijanian, young spectator's, puppet, youth Dramatic theatre, pantomime theatre, the theatre of musical comedies, and scores of other regional and amateur theatres which now operate in this country for our people.

These theatres have produced many brilliant actors and producers, such as Levon Kalantar and Arshak Burdjalian,

Hovhanness Abellian and Vahram Papazian, Hrachya Nersesian and Arus Voskanian, Mikael Manvelian and Avet Avetisian, Vagharsh Vagharshian and Armen Gulazian, Hasmik and Gurgen Djanibekian, Olga Gulazian and Vavik Vardanian, Vardan Adjemian and Hambartsum Khachanian, Armen Armenian, and Tsolak Amerikian; the famous singers Shara Talian and Haikanush Danielian, Gohar Gasparian and Tatevik Sazandarian, Lucineh Zakarian, Pavel Lisitsian and the master-teller Suren Kocharian...

It was on the stages of these theatres that the following enchanting classic works of the Armenian Opera and Ballet had their premières: Tigranian's *Anush* and *David Bek,* Spendarian's *Almast* and *Khandut,* Chukhajian's *Arshak II,* Khachaturian's *Gayaneh* and *Spartacus.*

The Philharmonic, Opera and Radio symphony orchestras, numerous musical bands and soloists have enabled Armenian music-lovers and the people as a whole to appreciate the music of Komitas, Kara-Murza, Yekmalian, Tigranian, Melikian, Stepanian, and the numerous talented young and middle-aged Armenian composers, thanks to whom the "Armenian school of music" is widely known beyond the borders of Armenia...

The works of Armenian painters, which have strayed from country to country since 1920 or fallen into the hands of private collectors, are now being gathered in their homeland for the first time.

Our people has been given the chance of seeing the precious treasures of Armenian painting and sculpture,

ranging from the medieval murals, khachkars (carved-stone crosses) and miniatures down to the works of talented contemporary Armenian painters and sculptors.

Armenia has more art galleries than most of the other republics of the USSR. Along with the well-known and rich collection of the State Art Gallery, many others have magically appeared such as the Modern Art Gallery, the Children's Gallery, the Union of Painters' Gallery, the House-Museums of Martiros Sarian, Hakop Kodjoyan, Ara Sarkisian, Harutyun Kalents and several mobile and district exhibitions.

The Armenian art galleries house numerous works by Russian artists and classics by world-famous masters and also the works of temporary Armenian artists living abroad.

The Yerevan State Art Gallery has original paintings by Tintoretto, Bassano, Donatello, Rubens, Van Dyke, Jordaens, Courbet, Fragonard and Gros.

Among the original works of 19th century Russian painters extibited here are Bryulov, Vershchagin, Makovsky, Kramskov, Surikov, Serov, Repin, Korovin, and among those of the 20th century, Petrov-Vodkin, Nesterov, Konchalovsky, Falk, Mashkovsky, Kandinsky, Chagall, and many others.

But the collecton of Armenian paintings is naturally the richest of all. It enables one to study the whole history of Armenian painting, as well as Armenian painting abroad from the works of Shahin, Gyurdjian, Pushman, Garzu and Orakian down to those of contemporary artists.

One may also make some unexpected discoveries even in the provincial galleries. Who would ever think that one could find the paintings of the contemporary American painter Rockwell Kent in Dilidjan? Or those of Grigor Sheldian, the outstanding contemporary Italian painter of Armenian extraction, in Etchmiadzin?

There are names of people who, each according to his era and style, reflect the best and most characteristic aspects of the cultural life of his people, people who may be proudly introduced to the world at large.

In Armenian painting they are Toros Roslin, Hakop Hovnatanian and Martiros Sarian.

The works of Toros Roslin, the 13th century Armenian painter of genius and supreme master of our medieval miniature painting, are its most vivid expression. He was not only a most remarkable master of intricate detail, but also an outstanding portrait painter who in many ways laid the foundations of the European Renaissance!

Hakop Hovnatanian's family tree in art begins with the famous Armenian poet and painter Naghash Hovnatan, who with his sons was the first to "transfer" the miniatures from manuscripts to the walls of the Cathedral of Etchmiadzin where he painted our first portraits — the images of the saints.

The most outstanding representative of the Hovnatanian family-tree undoubtedly was Hakop Hovnatianian who became the golden bridge between our medieval miniature art and that of modern times, thus laying the foundations of Armenian realist painting.

In 1922 the first state theatre named after Sundukyan
was founded in Yerevan...

He depicted a collective image of 19th century Armenian society, immortalizing not only the inner world and customs of representatives of its various strata, but also himself in unique canvases such as the portraits of Teumian, Nadirian and the Catholicos of all Armenians Nerses Ashtaraketsi...

As for Martiros Sarian, he was the first painter of our modern times, profoundly Armenian by character, to become widely celebrated the world over, thus putting Armenian painting on the world map, so to speak.

Sarian's sun, which shined in Armenian art for almost a century, warmed and "enlightened" us without dazzling us, and we were thus able to see more clearly and appreciate other traditions in our rich and multifaceted painting. Thus, we were able to appreciate Hovnatianian's wonderful bewildering naivity; Sureniants' paintings, imbibed with the history and spirit of the Armenians; Aivazovsky's seascapes; Bashindjaghian's landscapes; Aghadjanian's "Rembrandtian" portraits; Tadevosian's colourful dreams and impressions; Kodjoyan's miniatures and illustrations attaining a new peak in national art, and the masterful paintings of Arakelian and Bazhbeouk-Melikian...

Even if we had no others, Sarian alone would be powerful enough to make our contemporary painting world-famous.

But is Sarian the only one?

Only recently it was the wonderful sculptor Yervand Kochar, who with the magic wand of his talent brought to life David of Sassoun riding his faithful steed. In one leap David of Sassoun flew from the high Sassoun mountains of the ninth century down to the pedestal by the gates of Yerevan where he is the first of our people to welcome the guests entering the city...

And Hakop Kodjoyan, the outstanding master of graphic paintings, who has truly inherited all the best qualities of our medieval miniature art and given it new meaning and breath.

The bells heralding the revival of Armenia brought home not only many of the artists (both living and dead) from far-off lands but also many of their precious works.

In 1936, the ashes of the composer Komitas returned to Armenia. Driven insane by the horrors of the Armenian massacres, for twenty whole years Komitas suffered in psychiatric hospitals, first in Constantinople and then in Paris. It was only after his death that he was enabled to visit his revived homeland! His ashes were buried in Armenian soil like seeds which have now grown into fertile forests of Armenian music.

Together with (and like) the exiled people, the original score of the Opera of *Arshak II* by Tigran Chukhadjian returned home. For over a hundred years it had wandered through dusty archives, dreaming only of the stage of the Opera House in Armenia. The eternally youthful exquisite drawings of Edgar Shahin and the unique sculptures of Hakop Gyurdjian also returned home where they at last found a solid base in their native soil.

Many manuscripts and miniatures, ancient books and

archives, canvases and sculptures have returned to Armenia and are still doing so.

Among other paintings are the "Indian Pictures" by the Armenian refugee painter, Sarkis Khachaturian.

The son of a people who had lost their native land and arts after the Genocide of 1915, at a fairly advanced age he mustered enough strength to make a long and exhausting journey to India in order to save the art treasures of another people from ruin and to make them known to the world.

Clambering up mountains for many months he managed to get inside temples cut in the rocks and living on practically nothing, he copied the murals inside the temples which were being erased by winds and humidity.

Sometimes he hired Indian children who used a set of mirrors to reflect the sunlight into the cold dark caves so that he could make out the contours of the faded murals.

Even today some of these temples are hard to get to, not only for tourists but also for the Indians themselves, and many of the latter become acquainted with the murals thanks to the copies made by Sarkis Khachaturian...

In accordance with Sarkis Khachaturian's last testament, these paintings were transferred and the murals of several ancient Indian temples may only be studied in the Armenian capital...

Our astonishing people has had an equally astonishing fate.

So many pictures, sculptures, manuscripts, books, documents and archives have been "repatriated" that now at almost all the museums and galleries of Armenia there are special exhibition halls allotted to them.

At the appeal of our revived homeland, many skilled experts, doctors, scientists, actors, writers, singers and painters have returned home from abroad.

It is impossible to list them all, but some have to be mentioned: Gohar[1] Gasparian, the pearl in the crown of our songs; Kostan Zarian, one of the most original and modern writers of our century: conductor Hovhanness Chekidjian; Grigor Gurzadian, the cosmic scientist; the talented and original painters, Harutyun Kalents and Hakop Hakopian; singers Hovhanness Badalian and Mihran Yerkat; the actress Varduhi Varderesian; the architect Armen Zarian and many many others...

But there are also very many talented Armenian writers,, painters, scientists and specialists in many fields still living far away from their homeland, dreaming of it and devoting their skills to the foreign country they live in.

A few years ago, Rosy Armen, the talented Parisian variety singer of Armenian origin, gave a series of concerts in Yerevan.

Addressing the audience in her broken Armenian, the beautiful young Armenian girl had this to say:

"My father is Russian-Armenian, my mother — Turkish-Armenian, and I am French-Armenian..."

---

[1] Gohar is the word for 'pearl' in Armenian.

Three differeent kinds of Armenians in one family, under one roof, under an alien sky! Here are echoes of the tragedy of 1915 which are still heard to this day...

This is surely the reason why such talented people as the following live abroad: writer William Saroyan, Michael Arlen, Henry Troyat, Arthur Adamov, Vahe Kacha and Levon Surmelian, Alan Hovhanness, one of the most original composers of modern times, Charles Aznavour, the celebrated singer, poet and actor, Lily Chukasiszian and Lucy Amara, stars of the Metropolitan Opera House, poets Rouben Melik, Vahe Godel and Alicia Kirakosian, singer, Liz Pozapalian, photographers Hovsep Karsh and Haroutyun Kavukjian, popular singers, Silvi Vardan, Rosy Armen, and the painter Garzou.

And that's not to mention the numerous Armenian writers who in difficult conditions abroad wrote in their mother tongue, such as Hamastekh and Shahnoor who would have been worthy of any great literature of the 20th century.

To imagine the difficult position of Armenian writers abroad, one only has to remember the "advertisement" made by an Armenian writer in an Armenian newspaper published abroad.

After failing to sell a small number of a good book, which was published under great difficulties, the writer wrote an advertisement saying he was ready to send his books on request free of charge, so that they would at last be read and would not simply rot in a cellar.

Characteristically, no matter in what language Armenian writers happen to write or in what country they happen to live, their literary works, which are so dear to other peoples, express the historic fate of our people, its hopes and faith.

William Saroyan, one of the most prominent writers of modern times, wrote the following in the preface to one of his books:

"Although I write in English and am an American by birth, I consider myself an Armenian writer. The words I use are English, the environment I describe is America, but the spirit that makes me write is Armenian. Consequently, I am an Armenian writer".

What's more, sincerely regretting having been separated from his native language and literature, Saroyan never misses an opportunity to express his approval of the people whose work helps safeguard them.

The following inscription is printed on the title page of one of his books: "To Eghisheh Charents, Vahan Totovent and Gourgen Mahari—the poets, novellists and playwrights of Armenia, their children and grandchildren". During our meeting in Frezno he wrote in his own hand in the book he gave me: "And to writer Gevork Emin, who came from Ashtarak to Frezno, with admiration for a writer who, with his comrades keeps the Armenian language alive, young, vital, proud, beautiful and true.

sincerely
William Saroyan,
Frezno, Friday, December 24, 1971.

Amazed by our people's gift
for music...
Romain Rolland called Armenia
"Soviet Italy"...

This profound "Armenian" quality is felt in all creative Armenians abroad: in the poignant but optimistic and kind stories of William Saroyan, in the paintings in the cycle of the *Apocalypsis* of Garzu; in the dolefully sad "orphan" songs of Charles Aznavour, in the sounds of *The Sacred Mountain* of Alan Hovhanness and in many others.

Having absorbed the best of the spiritual culture of many peoples and countries beginning with Urartu, Persia and Hellas to the culture of the 20th century, our small but talented people has generously endowed the world with Roman philosophers, Byzantine monarchs and generals of Armenian origin, the delicious "Prunus Armeniaca" apricot, famous cochineal, the wonderful dome of the Cathedral of Aya Sophia and the extraordinary incipiency of the Gothic style; Dutch roses; the brilliant stories of William Saroyan and the splendid music of Aram Khachaturian.

... Amazed and delighted by our people's gift for music and true love and understanding of it, Romain Rolland called Armenia "Soviet Italy".

But until recently this "Italy", which has given the world so many talented musicians, minstrels and singers, didn't have a single music school or studio, not to mention a conservatory!

This might not seem very important to some and it is certainly easy nowadays not to pay any attention to it as Armenia has about forty musical, choreographic and art schools and colleges, the wonderful Conservatory, the

Institute of the Theatre and Arts at which over eight thousand talented young people study.

And one can't help wondering what Armenia would be like today if it hadn't these schools and colleges.

What would have become of the talented composer Arno Babadjanian, my old friend and contemporary, say, if he had been born, one hundred years ago in a remote Armenian village or in the provincial town of Yerevan with the same musical talent?

How many musically-gifted people like him would have at best become instrument players on national instruments at weddings, funerals and other public ceremonies?

How many of these instrument players are renowned today?

The same might have happened to Aram Khachaturian, yes, Aram Khachaturian, who turned the slow-moving cart of Armenian melodies into a jet of the 20th century, and gave the gentle stream of our folk songs the power and force of a stormy symphonic ocean whose waves are booming across the whole world.

And even if Khachaturian had managed to get a musical education and win recognition in a European country, how would the Armenian people have got to know his symphonies and brilliant concertos for violin, cello and piano? You see, the symphony orchestras, highly refined chamber orchestras, the wonderful Komitas String Quartet, and many other musical ensembles and soloists, which are so highly praised today, didn't exist then.

Who would ever be able to give back to the people the

wonderful folk songs and dances which have been bor-
rowed and beneficially used, if we didn't have our gifted
song and dance companies, and folk groups who are so
popular all over the world?

It may be possible to list all the professional musical
ensembles in Armenia today but it's quite impossible to do
the same with the amateur groups which operate in almost all the towns and villages, colleges and schools of
Armenia.

And how many "volcano eruptions" of talent among
the people are still to come!

Let's take, for instance, the amateur dance ensemble
of Sassoun from the village of Ashnak, founded by Vahram
Aristakesian. They are the same people of Sassoun about
whom Maxim Gorky once wrote as "a phenomenon of ex-
ceptional originality and beauty".

He could not even imagine of such an image of perfect
unity fused with dance rhythm and felt that this sort of
dance had originated from the remote past or it was the ri-
tual dance of pagan priests or the victory dance of the
warriors of Sassoun.

The spectators who knew nothing about the history of
the Armenians were simply amazed by the fiery dancing,
but the ones who knew our history even slightly, were
stunned and exclaimed: "Are there really any people of
Sassoun still alive? How could any of them have survived
those brutal massacres?" And by simply watching the
people of Sassoun dancing they all understood without
any explanation that:

... This wasn't a dance,
But the high cry of a country,
Where its people when defeated
Bear in their hearts the pride of it...
Where none could stalk
This ancient folk,
That knows to dance and makes one feel
Its charmful skill and dauntless will...!
They understood,
And heralded the world over!
Sassoun, indeed, so good for you,
Dance,
Dance,
You've still to see your dream come true,
And history — give back your due...
Dance,
Dance,
Meads are waiting your helping hand,
And the ploughs — to till the land...
Dance, till you see
All Armenians come in masses,
And weave this dance
At the foot-hills of Mount Massis...!

Ararat, or Mt. Massis, as the Armenians call it, one side of which is illuminated by the lights of Yerevan, while the other, the cradle of our people, is still deprived of Armenian light, songs and dances, arts and culture. It is as unknown and dark for us as the dark side of the Moon, except that we can at least see the Moon on television...

... It is a miracle to see so many new talents emerging

every day from the pages of books, from concert halls, exhibitions, buildings and harvests...

All this creative energy in the people, which has been suppressed for so many centuries, is now bursting out and finding creative and real fulfilment.

Many talents are following the footsteps of their predecessors and are still, in the process of being formed. Thousands of children are laying their fragile fingers on a piano key-board, or holding a violin bow, a pen, or drawing coloured crayons for the first time.

Every single Armenian, be he young or old, famous or not, joins in to the songs of Armenia, getting louder and louder every day and resounding throughout the world, telling people about our country and people.

Let our songs ring out across the world, and let the songs of all peoples of the world ring out in Armenia, for there is nothing nobler and finer than fraternity between peoples and songs.

... In recent years Armenian musical ensembles, actors, singers and readers have given many concerts to their brother Armenians abroad at which they are often requested to perform the song "Kroonk".

But this song is no longer the sad song of exiled people.

And the Armenians listening to it have also changed. They no longer beg for news from their distant suffering homeland. Now this song tells them about their revived homeland and calls them back to their nest...

The people's fate has changed, and so have their songs.

And after the victorious conclusion of the last World War, when the first Armenians were returning home. life itself inspired me to write my own version of "Kroonk".

Kroonk, your wings bore the ashes of Armenians
When you took flight...
You almost wept seeing the woes of Armenians,
When you took flight...
"I won't come back to your homeland... I see",— you said,
"Havoc and death...!"
And left your nest as desolate as our land,
And off you went...!
... Where had you been? You had your nest plundered again,
And back you came...
You had to cross through thousands of fires and swords,
But you were saved...
"One can't escape from death",— you said,— "I'd better die
In my old nest...!"
And turned your eyes to the bright peaks of **Ararat,**
And back you came...
You came and saw new waterlines were being laid
Through the deserts...
Roses blooming on every stone, and stone buildings
Climbing the sky...
Life growing brighter, smokes curling up, and birds heading.
Back to their nests...
You came and brought only the grief of refugees,
Upon your wings...
You came to find your nest restored, and you flew back
To foreign lands,
So as to save your own babes from the black blight
And utter loss...!
... Then, on you go, from land to land and return back,
Welcome to you!

Go and call up the refugees, and return back,
Welcome to you!
Be well aware that none of them should have to wait
Too long for you...
Or start to weep and say: "Kroonk, some news for me...!"
Welcome to you...!

The refugees are now coming back to their homeland
on their own and with their families from towns and
villages, by car, by train, plane and, most of all, by ship...

And these ships pass through the straits of the Bosphorus, from the shores of which other ships loaded with
refugees left for foreign lands in 1915!

They come ...the victims saved from the slaughters...!
And how pleased would the Bosphorus be,
To have clenched the jaws of its lewd waters,
And have them drowned in the bloody sea...!

And yet times have changed, and so has the fate
Of all Armenians who now make haste
To sail back... on board the ship "Armenia",
Closely escorted by the liner "Russia".

As they cross the straits in jubilant mood,
Heading to their land to settle for good,
The Bosphorus gapes with jaws wide open,
Seeing in all this... an aweful omen...!

About three hundred thousand exiled Armenians have
already returned to their homeland, giving six hundred
thousand hands to help build a new life in our land.

And those who haven't returned for good, came as

tourists and guests just to see their motherland. Every year we are visitied by many Armenian tourist groups, delegations, writers, artists, composers and singers. The visits by large groups of specialists, such as doctors, engineers and teachers, have now become traditional. Teachers at Armenian schools abroad, for instance, spend their holidays in Armenia attending lectures, meeting scientists, writers and other teachers, and sightseeing.

At the same time their pupils spend their holidays together in the most beautiful summer camps of Armenia.

One summer, I witnessed an unforgettable scene in one of these camps.

It was the visiting Armenian children's last evening at the camp. After calling the children together the camp leader bade them farewell: "Dear friends, we sang and danced together today for the last time. You're leaving tomorrow..." Then, suddenly law and order collapsed and the children rushed up to one another, embracing and kissing each other... and exclaiming first in a low voice and then louder and louder: "No, no, we don't want to leave, we won't, we won't..."

Law and order at the camp collapsed for the first time. Till late into the night in the dormitories the boys kept exclaiming something excitedly while the girls cried either in the arms of their "local" friends or with their heads in their pillows...

It was especially hard for the adults because there was nothing they could do or say. Words had no power over this omnipotent surge of emotion. And how and why should

Go and call up the refugees,
and return back...

they leave when they had been given not a fantastic or-imaginative but a real fairy-land—their homeland!

People, books, paintings and songs are returning home. The torn pages of manuscripts and books, fragments of the same pictures and sculptures are now uniting the two halves of a people who have suffered so much.

But how many centuries are needed to gather everyone under one roof?

Yes, many relatives and friends are still looking for one another. All the Armenian papers all over the world are full of announcements written by people searching for relatives and friends.

Most people are born, live and work in the same country. But this is not true for two million Armenians They may have been born in Western Armenia, say, think of their homeland as Soviet Armenia and live somewhere in Beirut or New-York.

And every day in front of the *Armenia* and *Ani* hotels in Yerevan, Armenian tourists are surrounded by crowds of people asking after their lost relatives and friends.

And if another song were to be added to these songs about Armenia, it would be called the Song of a Dream Come True, a dream which was dreamed not by one person for one night, but by a whole people for centuries.

This song has only just begun and will go on being sung for a long time to qome.

After all, this new regeneration of nations whose influence is being felt all over our multinational homeland, means that bitter errors and injustices of history will be put right and the most cherished dreams of peoples will come true. And this is surely true of our people known as the "long-suffering Armenians".

The exiled will return to become legal owners of their native land and their new life... and then, as great Toumanian wrote at the dawn of the century:

> And the poets who never brewed
> Their lips in curse, falsehood, and hiss,
> Will hail and praise your life renewed,
> With merry songs and words of bliss,
> My new homeland,
> My mighty land...!

Yes, the poets will praise the new life of their new country.

Their country which for centuries has suffered from wars and invasions and has only recently felt the sweetness of peaceful life and work.

Their stony country which has at last cast off the stones of age-long suffering and is using them to build new homes.

Their country whose mountain rivers have for centuries raging and roaring in idleness and only recently have been used to give light and make fertile the land.

Their country whose soil has for centuries been watered only by bitter blood and sweat and only recently has begun yielding fruit.

Their country, born out of flames, in which for centuries cruel fires have blazed and in which only recently the beneficial   fires of blast-furnaces and factories keep always glowing.

Their country of ancient manuscripts whose ancient letters record the behests of a new life and bright future.

And, finally, their country, whose songs, which were once lost in the mountains, are now hovering over foreign lands like cranes and resounding all over the world!

COLOPHON BY THE AUTHOR OF THIS BOOK

That was the last, seventh song about Armenia...

Everything in life has a beginning and an end, but a people and their songs can surely go on forever...!

I, Gevorg Emin, son of Grigor, a vine-grower from the village of Ashtarak, and Arusyak, a weaver from the province of Goghtan, and, the son of all the Armenian people, have related only what I have read in ancient Armenian manuscripts and modern books, what I have heard from my ancestors and contemporaries, seen with my own eyes and created with my own hands, and I call upon the future poets of Armenia to continue the unfinished lines of these songs which are as eternal as life itself.

But life goes on. Yesterday about 150 boys and girls were born at the maternity homes of Yerevan and added their powerful voices to the ancient song of Armenia.

They still haven't been given names but whether its Vahan, Grigor, Artuit or Alik they are known to us by only one name — Galik, or the future.

May they grow up and inherit this land of ours which has come to us from the distant past and will continue into the distant future. This long-suffering but happy land of ours which is small but bountiful in dreams, and whose shining crest bears the following:

Mount Ararat — the witness of our centuries-old history!

The Vine and Ear of Corn, which have grown on this land since the time of Patriarch Noah!

The Hammer and Sickle — the eternal symbols of peaceful work!

And the Sun — the Red Sun, under whose rays the Armenian people has lived, continues to live and will always live...!

GEVORG EMIN
Seven Songs About Armenia

ԳԵՎՈՐԳ ԷՄԻՆ
Յոթ երգ Հայաստանի մասին

ГЕВОРГ ЭМИН Семь песень об Армении (На английском языке) Издательство «Советакан грох» Ереван. 1983.

Հրատ. խմբագիր՝ Ա. Ս. Հովսեփյան, գեղ. խմբագիր՝ Վ. Ա. Հարություն-
յան, տեխ. խմբագիր՝ Ս. Մ. Սիմոնյան, վերատտուգող սրբագրիչներ՝
Մ. Հ. Սողիկյան, Ա. Ս. Հովսեփյան

ИБ № 3255.
Հանձնված է շարվածքի 5. 05. 1981 թ.։ Ստորագրված է տպագրության
8. 08. 1983 թ.։ Ֆորմատ՝ 70×108¹/₃₂։ Թուղթ՝ կավճապատ։ Տառատե-
սակ՝ «Լատինական»։ Տպագրություն՝ բարձր։ 15,75 պայմ. տպ. մամ.,
16,14 պայմ. ներկ. ըերթ, 16,4 Հրատ. մամ.։ Պատվեր 870։ Տպաքանակ
10000։ Գինը 2 ռ. 90 կ.։
«Սովետական գրող» Հրատարակչություն, Երևան—9, Տերյան 91։
Изд-во «Советакан грох», Ереван-9, ул. Теряна, 91.
ՀՍՍՀ Հրատարակչությունների, պոլիգրաֆիայի և գրքի առևտրի գործերի
պետական կոմիտեի № 1 տպարան, Երևան, Ալավերդյան 65։
Типография № 1 Госкомитета по делам издательств, полиграфии
и книжной торговли, Арм. ССР. Ереван, ул. Алавердяна 65.